Praise for
can I kiss you?

"Can I Kiss You? may be one of the most important books you ever read. Mike Domitrz's important work changes, and saves, lives! Read this book; then re-read it. And make sure to get copies for anyone you love and care about."

— *James Malinchak, Featured on ABCs Hit TV Show,* Secret Millionaire, *Co-Author of the Best-Selling book,* Chicken Soup for the College Soul

"As a sergeant who supervised the San Diego Police Department Sex Crimes Unit for ten years and the founder of End Violence Against Women International, I am painfully aware of the need for this book and the outreach Michael J. Domitrz has with young people. When I read the book, I immediately thought, "I want my nineteen-year-old daughter, a university freshman, to read this." The book isn't just for young people who are exploring healthy relationships and intimacy. It can also be extremely helpful for parents and other family members who should be talking to the young adults in their lives about healthy relationships and potential abuse. Professionals such as teachers, social workers, counselors, and law enforcement will also find the information useful. I highly recommend adding Can I Kiss You? to your reading list."

— *Joanne Archambault, Executive Director, EVAW International*

"Can I Kiss You? is an excellent read whether you are twelve or have been married sixty years. You'll be challenged to examine your own relationship and how you communicate with others. This book is insightful and gives practical ways to deal with awkward dating situations and human interaction while incorporating themes of respect and honesty throughout."

— *Ms. Sarah Sullivan, Educator, Military Victim Advocate, and Veteran*

i

"Can I Kiss You? is more than a sexual assault book—it is more than a dating book. Its pages are filled with valuable life-saving scenarios, questions, and solutions; it will empower you with heightened awareness that could save your life or the life of someone you know!"

> — *Becky Mackintosh, Author, Speaker, Teacher, Mother, and Grandmother*

"Domitrz's Can I Kiss You? is one of the greatest resources regarding respect, consent, and relationships. Filled with knowledge, examples, interactive exercises, and links to web-based resources, this book will be useful to anyone seeking guidance in developing healthy relationships, parents wishing to address more than the physical element of the 'birds and the bees,' and educators wanting to reduce rates of sexual violence."

> — *Eric S. Davidson, PhD, MCHES, CSPS, Director of Illinois Higher Education Center for Alcohol, Other Drug, and Violence Prevention*

"Can I Kiss You? elevates our relationships to a higher moral personal value code."

> — *Jessica Pettitt, Diversity Educator & Author*

"Can I Kiss You? is a 'must read' for parents, students, and educators. Mike Domitrz breaks through the confusion of body language and assumptions to provide every student with clear, specific skill sets for building healthy, respectful, and wonderful relationships."

> — *Ida Echevarria NYC Board of Education, Retired Director of Testing and Assistant Superintendent*

"Mike Domitrz has provided a terrific resource for anyone who wants to think more deeply about the issues of respect, consent, sexual assault, and anti-violence activism. *Can I Kiss You?* covers all the territory in language accessible to students, parents, teachers, and anyone else who wants to be a part of the solution when it comes to contributing to an atmosphere of respect and inclusion."

> — *Christopher Kilmartin, Ph.D., Professor of Psychological Science, University of Mary Washington*

"Can I Kiss You? breaks new ground by sensitively examining every aspect of physical intimacy from "The Look" to "The Morning After." With gentle humor and a deft hand, Mike Domitrz gracefully walks us through the newest issues in this age-old topic. Without condescension or judgment, Mike gives our children the tools they need to grow up sensible, strong, and healthy and with a better appreciation of what makes them—and their partner—comfortable, happy, and content."

> — *David Altshuler, M.S. and Author of* Love the Kid You Get. Get the Kid You Love

"Can I Kiss You? shifts the focus of our conversation about consent away from what is or is not legal behavior. At its root, the act of asking to be intimate is about respect—respect for self and for others. Rather than wonder, "Do I have to ask?" readers recognize their desire to ask and be asked, and anything less is now disrespectful. This book is a primer for building the confidence and skills needed to have healthy relationships."

> — *Jackie Deitch-Stackhouse, Director for the Sexual Harassment/ Assault Advising, Resources, and Education (SHARE) Office at Princeton University*

"Confusion and disregard as it pertains to personal boundaries borders on an epidemic. This is why *Can I Kiss You?* should be required reading for anyone 9-90."

> — *Robert Siciliano, Safety Expert and CEO of IDTheftSecurity.com*

"While this book is little and geared to all ages, the cultural paradigm shift Mike suggests is profound. If our current cultural glamorizing of Game/Boss/Baller could shift to one of demonstrating confidence and respect through asking permission—even for a kiss, our world would be a much safer place. This book is a fantastic conversation starter and can be considered useful in forums ranging from classrooms to bedrooms."

> — *Yvette Currie, Licensed Marriage and Family Therapist, Deployed Resiliency Counselor*

"*Can I Kiss You?* is direct, easy to understand, full of great insights, and a guide for why and how to ask. I am putting this book on the 'must read' list for both parents and students for our middle schools and high schools to help them better understand the dynamics of relationships."

— *Margo Chevers, Coordinator, Tri-Town Domestic Violence Task Force*

"*Can I Kiss You?* is filled with lesson plans and creative approaches to consent education. I can't imagine doing a consent presentation without using something I've read in this book!"

— *Kristen Altenau Keen, Sexual Violence Prevention Education Coordinator, University of Dayton*

"*Can I Kiss You?* will provide hours of great conversation about sexual assault and how we can have a positive impact on stemming the ever-growing tide of new victims and offenders."

— *Tim Meacham, University of Richmond Police Office and Educator of Sexual Assault Awareness*

"This amazing book bravely and courageously goes where no book has gone before. It provokes ideas and discussions about relationships and intimacy that are so compelling it should be required reading in every classroom in the country. Highly interactive, parents, educators, and students will find insight, inspiration, and encouragement on every page. As a mother of four grown daughters, I only wish I had read this book sooner."

— *Stacy Allegro, Mom and Author*

"Mike's message is so powerful for anyone at any age wanting to explore how to communicate with respect while dating or being intimate with others. Can I Kiss You? is more than a book about sexual assault awareness; it's an empowering personal development book that will change your life."

— *Berni Xiong, Intuitive Branding Coach and Reiki Master*

"Can I Kiss You? is a wonderful tool for pre-teens to adults. It is such an easy read and brings a different light to healthy relationships to include consent, respect, and intervention techniques. I use it for myself, my children, and in prevention training as an educator and victim's advocate."

— *Ms. Jamie Cram, Mom, Educator, and Victim Advocate*

"*Can I Kiss You?* is filled with examples and practical activities to help you have the often unconquerable conversations about kissing, sex, and more—before things get out of control. A must read book for everyone, all genders and sexual orientations, who want to make sure the relations they have are truly consensual."

— *Phil Gerbyshak, Speaker and Author of* 10 Ways to Make It Great

"This book is about reducing sexual assault, but also about building healthy and fulfilling relationships, learning and practicing effective communication skills, building self-respect, and creating a better world. Domitrz skillfully incorporates the most recent research and thinking in gender and sexuality into a text that is accessible, practical, and effective."

— *Tal Peretz, Assistant Professor of Sociology and Women's Studies, Auburn University*

"As someone who's been working with feminist collectives and women's support groups in a country torn by sexist traditions, I found *Can I Kiss You?* to be a source of useful information and strategies to deal with abusive relationships and sexual assault. It is a required read for anyone interested in building a safer, more equal, and respectful world."

— *Henrique Marques Samyn, Professor at the State University of Rio de Janeiro (UERJ), Brazil*

"Michael Domitrz hits the mark with this book! As a parent, physician, and educator for over thirty years, I have seen how communication can change our lives. Michael's insight and expertise on this topic is second to none!"

— *Dr. Rick Goodman, CSP*

"*Can I Kiss You?* is a great primer on consent in dating and intimate relationships. Mike has an ability to explain things in simple and accessible ways that are also powerful and memorable. He not only describes ways of communicating and interacting, but he also points out the absurdity of not doing so. This great resource is inclusive of all kinds of relationships for those wanting to learn about consent and those who want to teach others about it—including parents and educators of all kinds."

> — *Keith E. Edwards, PhD, Leadership Coach, Speaker, and Consultant on College Men, Sexual Assault Prevention, and Social Justice Education*

"Don't let the title fool you. *Can I Kiss You?* is more than a guidebook on how to navigate dating and sex for youth. It shows readers of all ages how to navigate healthy boundaries in long-term relationships as well as practical tips on effectively supporting survivors of sexual assault. College Residence Life and Counseling Staff should integrate the principles of this book to improve campus safety and overall student health."

> — *Jennifer L. FitzPatrick, MSW, LCSW-C, CSP, Adjunct Instructor, Johns Hopkins University*

"*Can I Kiss You?* is an insightful breakdown of the often complex issues relating to relationships. It offers examples to overcome both misunderstandings and even blatant manipulation in dating. As a former investigator, assigned to a police Sensitive Crimes Unit, I have a special appreciation and respect for all aspects of Mike's mission, which begins with the pertinent information contained in this most important book."

> — *Detective Rick Haines (Ret), Sensitive Crimes Unit, Waukesha Police Department*

can
I kiss
you?

can
I kiss
you?

A Thought-Provoking Look at
Relationships, Intimacy & Sexual Assault

Michael J. Domitrz

This publication is designed to provide accurate and authoritative information with regard to the subject matter covered. It is sold with the understanding that the publisher is not engaged in rendering legal, accounting, or other professional advice. If legal advice or other expert assistance is required, the services of a competent professional person should be sought.

—From a Declaration of Principles jointly adopted by a Committee of the American Bar Association and a Committee of Publishers and Associations

Can I Kiss You? A Thought-Provoking Look at Relationships, Intimacy & Sexual Assault, is a trademark of The Date Safe Project, Inc, Awareness Publications, and Michael J. Domitrz, denoting a series of products that may include but are not limited to books (paper, digital, audio, electronic, video), pocket cards, and calendars.

Edited by: Tyler Tichelaar and Carolyn Kott Washburne

Cover and text design by: wisnet.com LLC

ISBN: 978-0-9972866-0-1

Library of Congress Control Number: 2016934391

Printed in the United States of America

First Printing 2016

20   19   18   17   16   6   5   4   3   2   1

Publisher's Cataloging-in-Publication Data

Domitrz, Michael J.

Can I Kiss You? A Thought-Provoking Look at Relationships, Intimacy & Sexual Assault/ Michael J. Domitrz. 1st ed.   Milwaukee, WI : Awareness Publications, 2016.
p. cm.
ISBN
1. Man-woman relationships. 2. Dating (social customs)
3. Interpersonal communication. 4. Communication and sex. 5. Rape prevention.

HQ801 .D66 2003
306.73—dc21

Published by

▲
Awareness
Publications
P.O. Box 20906 • Greenfield WI 53220-0906
800-329-9390 • www.awarenesspublications.com

This book is available at quantity discounts.
For information, call 800-329-9390.

With Special Thanks

To my family and supporters who believed in me and helped me write my first book in 2003, your early and continued support has helped us reach millions of people over the past decade: Joan Domitrz (Mom), Joe Domitrz (Dad), Janet Simkus, Paul Simkus, Peter Browne, Scott Thomas, and Ed Wegner. To my two aunts who were big believers in our work and have since passed away: Marilyn Hamilton and Kay Lewis. To my cousin, Bryan, you helped us build a larger online presence.

To my friends and colleagues who encouraged me to speak and live my mission, you inspired me to take those first steps into founding The Date Safe Project and speaking full-time: Patty Hendrickson, Randy Haveson, Jerry Witherill, Joseph Weinberg, David Avrin, Sean Stephenson, Victor Gonzalez, and Michael Karpovich.

To my first publishing team in 2003, you helped bring my best voice forward: Nick Laird, Susan Pittelman, and Georgene Schreiner. For the many experts who helped bring great insight to the discussions in my writings, thank you! Alan Berkowitz, your contributions to the book have helped countless readers. Carolyn Kott Washburne, Rose Rezaei, Jo Jones, Joanne Archambault, and Tyler Tichelaar, your suggestions and brilliance in the editing process were wonderful.

To the wisnet team that helped bring the messages of this book to the cover and throughout the layout, your artistry and genius shines through.

To my close confidants, your guidance and wisdom is a never-ending gift: Sam Silverstein, Chad Hymas, Ruby Newell-Legner, Ed Gerety, and Jessica Pettitt.

To the Dream Team I get the honor of working with every day here at The Date Safe Project, Inc., you rock! Rita, you have been on this journey with me for the past thirteen years, helping us to reach millions around the world. From the early years to today, you have been a Rock Star! None of my speaking or writing would be possible without the amazing team at home: my wife and four sons. Thank you for your patience, support, understanding, inspiration, and love.

To my incredible sister, Cheri

Thank you for your strength, courage, and love.
You have been the inspiration behind all of my work.
You continue to be a model for all survivors.

I love you, Cheri!

Contents

Introduction

Have you ever been on a date? Do you plan on dating? Are you single? Are you married with children? Do you know a student or an educator? Do you know other human beings? That pretty much covers the whole gamut of society, doesn't it? If you answered, "Yes" to any of these questions, this book is for you!

Educators want a book students can relate to, a book that inspires individuals to act with more respect toward one another, a book that serves as a continual resource for simple answers to tough questions.

Parents want a book to help them talk with their children about dating and intimacy.

Teenagers and adults want honest and down-to-earth solutions they can use without feeling embarrassed.

From this demand, *Can I Kiss You?* was written. Whether you have never dated, have been dating for years, or are married, this book will challenge you to evaluate the beliefs society has taught us about dating, communication, and respect.

While reading this book, you will relate to many situations. At the same time, you may find yourself saying, "I never looked at it that way before." Once you see the new perspective, you will want to make a change—a change you didn't expect.

The Inspiration

In the fall of 1989, my world abruptly halted when I received a devastating call from my mom. My sister had been raped. Over the next two years, everything I believed about dating was challenged.

My own self-worth was questioned. I went from wanting to kill my sister's rapist to looking at myself in the mirror and saying, "Who am I to judge?"

I asked my friends, "How do you date?" and soon learned that the more assertive partners' actions on a date were not far from the motivations of a serial rapist. The assertive partners were assuming what the other person wanted and then acting upon their own assumptions. At the same time, our society was teaching the passive individuals to accept this unhealthy dating culture. A change was desperately needed.

After hearing a speaker on sexual assault address the school I was attending, a realization struck me. Each person can make a difference! I gathered all of the information I could on the subject of sexual assault. Then I researched, researched, and did some more research. With all this knowledge, I created an interactive program on dating, communication, and respect to help reduce the occurrence of sexual assault.

Educators and students told me people needed to hear my challenging and life-changing message. Today, I travel the world, sharing the lessons in this book with people of all ages, genders, sexual orientations, and socioeconomic backgrounds!

Why "Can I Kiss You?"

If you are a reader of my first book, *May I Kiss You?*, you might be wondering why the new version of the book is titled *Can I Kiss You?*

I always wanted the title of the original book to be *Can I Kiss You?* At the time, educational consultants had argued that "Can I Kiss You?" would be grammatically incorrect because people have the ability to kiss someone whether they ask or not. I disagreed. Why?

A person does not have the legal ability to touch people sexually without their permission. As we will discuss later, sexually touching someone without the person's consent is sexual assault. Therefore, you do not have the legal ability to kiss someone without asking first.

Why does this matter? If you believed people have the legal ability to kiss or engage in sexual activity without mutual agreement of the persons involved, you are more likely to have people believing they can do whatever they want to others—agreement or not.

The second reason for changing the title is this book has a lot of new content, including new concepts and skill sets being taught.

What's Inside

Can I Kiss You? is about more than sexual assault. You will find the pages filled with challenging questions, thought-provoking scenarios, dynamic solutions, and life-changing philosophies. While you can find books detailing research and statistics, *Can I Kiss You?* provides a unique perspective.

The characters mentioned throughout the book rarely are labeled with a specific gender or sexual orientation. People of all gender identities, forms of expression, and romantic orientations should be able to see themselves and/or those they care about in each situation. Individuals who are not dating or in a relationship also need to see themselves. For this reason, names are not specific to a gender. In addition, the pronouns "they" and "them" are used throughout the book.

How you read this book can be impacted by your personal experience and culture. When asked to take actions or engage in conversations at certain points in the book, please consider how to do so in a way that best fits you.

In *Can I Kiss You?*, a **date** is defined as partners with an intimate attraction (and/or considering an intimate attraction) spending time together. A date can include a first date, a couple hanging out (single or committed), a "hook-up" and/or a group of couples spending time together.

Can I Kiss You? is an in-depth look at dating, relationships, intimacy, communication, respect, and sexual assault. Throughout this book, you will find specific actions you can take to make a positive impact in your life and in the lives of those you care about. If you understand the concepts in this book and then live your life accordingly, you will feel more empowered while dating. You will experience healthier intimacy in your current and future relationships.

The added benefit? You will thrive in relationships with a greater awareness of yourself and your partner. By doing so, you will help reduce the number of uncomfortable dating situations. You will help reduce the number of sexual assaults occurring in the world.

When you choose to be sexually intimate, you will help increase the likelihood of you and your partner experiencing mutually amazing consensual intimacy.

Are you ready? You are about to take a journey that will cause you to laugh, think quietly, and look in the mirror. Let the reading begin!

Are You Average?

What does "average" mean? Do you respond in dating situations the same way most people would respond? As you read this book, decide when and how you fit the following statements:

- In some situations, I follow the norms of dating.
- In some situations, I defy the norms of dating.

Each person can provide a different answer for every question in this book. To keep the book concise, fun to read, and powerful, we will be taking a close look at the "average" response given by a person.

When your answer is different from the average, do not be disappointed. Unique results can be positive. Simply recognize why your answer was different, and then ask yourself, "Is this good, or should I make a change?" As you read the book, you will learn how to tell the difference.

On the average date, how does the way you respect your partner and communicate with your partner relate to behaviors associated with sexual assault? In spending time with people from around the world, I have never met people who believed they intentionally assaulted a dating partner. People do not notice their own behaviors until they are given a new perspective. Once people's eyes are opened to the realities of dating, they share their stories of confusion, disrespect, and assault.

No one is immune to this important societal problem. I believed "I was not the type, nor were my friends" and "I could never sexually assault someone"—until the day my mom called to tell me that my sister had been raped. That call changed my life and inspired me to make changes.

No professional or expert can guarantee 100 percent prevention of sexual assault or unhealthy dating situations. However, the more prepared you are with knowledge and awareness, the more you can help.

Can I Kiss You? is full of direct and upfront conversation concerning dating, communication, respect, sexual intimacy, and sexual assault. The questions and issues you will be challenged with exist in all types of dating and intimate relationships. So—Are you ready for a challenge?

1

The Look
You Know What I Mean

Have you ever felt nervous about dating? Do you wonder what your date is going to think of you? Do you worry about how the date is going to end? To understand dating, the dangers involved, and how to build wonderful relationships, we must first comprehend the way we communicate on dates.

Body language is the most common form of communication in dating. For example, do most people ask before they kiss someone? No. Instead, they try to figure out when is the right time to make their "move." How do they figure out when is the right time? By reading body language.

The world of dating relies heavily on sending and receiving body language signals. Is body language reliable? No. If it were, you would know when someone wanted to be intimate with you. You would never experience confusing moments in the beginning of intimacy or during intimacy. You would always know how comfortable your partner was with you. Occurrences of sexual assaults could be greatly reduced by effective communication.

Are you good at reading body language? Are you great at sending the right "messages" to your dates? Take this Body Language Challenge. If you have a group of people, each of you take the test individually and then share your answers.

TAKING THE BODY LANGUAGE CHALLENGE

Challenge No. 1: Imagine you are single. An attractive person is sitting across the room from you. Send the person messages through your body language to tell them you want to ask them out on a date. Will the person interpret your signals perfectly? For a fun exercise, try this with another person. Remember, this person has to interpret your body language correctly.

Challenge No. 2:
Write down all of the body language signals used by individuals on a date to communicate with each other. Include every signal imaginable. Example: moving closer to someone to let the person know you like them.

Challenge No. 3:
A couple, Dakota and Casey, are walking down the beach together on a date. As they hold hands, Dakota can feel that Casey's hands are sweaty and holding on tightly. Write down how Dakota is likely to read Casey's signals. Next, write down what feelings Casey might be experiencing to cause the tight grip and sweaty palms.

Challenge No. 4:
During a date, Dakota is having a great time and really likes Casey. The two of them are sitting closely together. To send a message of being attracted to Casey, Dakota places a hand on Casey's knee. Write how you think Casey will read this signal from Dakota. Be detailed in your answer.

Challenge No. 5:
Have you ever heard someone say, "When he/she gave me 'the look,' I just knew what he/she wanted?" People often refer to the "look"

when describing romantic moments. How would you describe your version of the "look"? Write a detailed description of the look you would give another person to let them know you are interested. Ask a friend to try this challenge and then share your answers with each other.

Challenge No. 6:

Write down the amount of time two people can exhaust trying to read each other's body language before one tries to kiss the other. Example: Dakota and Casey are alone and sitting together in a private place. Both of them want to kiss each other, but they are not verbally asking. They are making conversation while trying to read each other's body language. How much time could pass before one of them actually tries to kiss the other?

Have you completed all six steps of the Body Language Challenge? Each of the challenges are real situations that can occur every day of the week. Let's see how well you did.

DISCUSSING THE BODY LANGUAGE CHALLENGE

Challenge No. 1:

If you tried this challenge with another person, did either of you laugh? The reason people will start laughing during this exercise is because each of you realizes how silly you look trying to send body language signals. While trying to read another person's body language, you feel like you are trying to read the person's mind. Reading minds is a skill most people admit they don't possess. If you can't read minds, body language does not work.

For body language to be an effective means of communication, everyone needs to use the same "signals." Since every person reads "signals" differently, you cannot guarantee the correct interpretation of body language.

Challenge No. 2:

Are you done writing all the body language signals? For fun, share the answers with other people. If you wrote down every possible body language signal, you would be writing for days (flirting for fun, letting a person know you are attracted to them, sending the signal you want to kiss, etc.). Since an infinite number of "signals" exists, knowing all of them is impossible.

Challenge No. 3:

Dakota's Reaction: "If Casey is holding my hand tightly, Casey likes me. Casey is letting me know how enjoyable holding my hand is. Casey might even have strong feelings for me. The sweaty palms are telling me Casey is nervous and wants everything to go right . . . another sign Casey really likes me."

Casey's Reaction: "My hands are sweaty because I am nervous. Dakota has made some comments during the date that make me feel uncomfortable. In fact, I am a little scared being alone with Dakota as we walk down the beach. I want to pull my hand away from Dakota, but I don't know how Dakota will react. I don't want to get Dakota mad, especially with us being all alone out here. I was holding Dakota's hand tightly? I didn't even notice. Must have been my nerves." Dakota and Casey were experiencing the exact same body language, yet each had completely different reactions to Casey's signals. These misunderstandings can happen on any date.

 How about this?

Write down situations in which a person could misread a date's body language. Be specific on how the person could misread the body language. In many cases, you could have multiple possibilities for interpreting the same body language.

Example

In Challenge No. 3, what else could Casey have been trying to tell Dakota? How else could Dakota have read Casey's body language?

Challenge No. 4:

Will Dakota think, "Oh, how nice. Casey is touching my knee to let me know Casey is interested in me"? More likely, Dakota will think, "Yes! Casey wants me!" Dakota may start to believe Casey wants them to become highly sexually involved (more than kissing).

Is there a difference between "liking" a partner and "wanting" a partner? The difference can be gigantic and can lead to tremendous assumptions and problems. Challenge No. 4 shows how one commonly used body language signal can lead to confusion and misunderstanding.

Challenge No. 5:

Did you find it hard to describe your "look"? If you shared the description of your "look" with a friend, were either of you laughing? The reality is that one standard "look" does not exist. Every person has a completely different "look." To understand another person's "look," everyone would have to know each other's distinct expressions, and each expression could only have one meaning.

If body language worked, you would know precisely what a partner was thinking when he/she gave you a "look." On a date, one partner would always know whether the other partner wanted to kiss. Either partner could send a look to tell the way he/she liked being kissed. You would know precisely how far your partner wanted to go. All of this information just from a "look"? Is that possible? No.

Picture Jess walking into a party where tons of people are crammed in the room. After being at the party for a while, Jess scopes out the crowd and notices one gorgeous individual, Skylar. This person is everything Jess wants in a partner. As Jess's eyes are stuck gazing upon this person, the gorgeous individual turns. Yes. Skylar looks over Jess's way. This moment is the very opportunity Jess has been waiting for. Jess gives a nod toward Skylar as Jess smiles with a look of, "Hey, how are you doing?" smacked across Jess's face. A smile comes across Skylar's face—as if Skylar had been waiting to see Jess.

Jess feels incredible. Jess turns to a friend, Dallas, in a voice filled with nervous energy, and says, "Did you see the gorgeous one looking at me? Did you see that smile? I think I am being checked out." Dallas starts smirking and says, "Do you mean the one over there?" "Yes, exactly," says Jess. Dallas replies, "The same one waving and smiling to the person right behind you?" Jess turns and realizes Skylar was not looking at them. Skylar was looking at another person who was standing behind Jess's group of friends.

Does the above scenario happen? Yes, every day of the week, to thousands of people. Embarrassing? Most definitely, and most of us have experienced this type of humiliation (at school, a concert, a party, etc.).

Why do we think the person is looking at us? Because being recognized in a positive manner feels good. Being wanted creates an even more powerful rush. When we interpret body language, we often project our hopes and wants onto the other person. By doing so, we see what we *want* to see.

 How about this?

Have you ever enjoyed helping another person, but then the person thought you were attracted to them? Why did the person think you were attracted to them? Many times, people assume someone being nice to another person is a sign of attraction.

Write down specific examples of how this can happen at work or school or with a group of friends. How do you react when the person misunderstands your "being nice"? What is the most respectful way you could react in these situations?

Example

Taylor is helping Kendall, a classmate, with homework. They are laughing and having a great time together. Kendall goes home and tells friends that the two of them had a connection and are now attracted to each other. When Taylor finds out, Taylor is surprised by Kendall's version of what happened. Taylor did not feel an attraction.

When Skylar looked toward Jess, Jess wanted Skylar to desire Jess and so Jess believed that Skylar did. When you are on a date, you want to believe that the other person finds you attractive. You look for signs confirming the attraction. Here is the problem. You are *looking* for signs showing the person is attracted to you. By doing so, your mind can interpret any sign as a positive sign, a sign of attraction. Everyone subconsciously participates in this progression of thoughts.

This projection of thoughts and wants can be extremely harmful in dating situations and relationships. Once you think the other person wants something, you might go after it. You make an intimate move on your partner (a form of sexual contact) because you assume this person wants it. However, the person didn't want it. Now, you have sexually assaulted your date. How? As we'll discuss later when defining sexual assault, you didn't have consent. This danger is why relying on body language is a horrible way to communicate.

Challenge No. 6:
How much time did you think would pass before a kiss was attempted? From five minutes to over two hours is the common answer to this challenge. A college student once told me, "I waited the entire date. I just kept waiting for my date to kiss me, and he never did."

If body language worked, you would only take seconds to know the "right time" to kiss. Why don't we know in just seconds? Because reading another person's body language is problematic. In fact, it is a guess. Whether you wait five minutes or two hours to read someone's signals before you make your move to kiss, will you then know for certain the other person wants to kiss? No, you will not. *Unless you directly ask, you are always taking a guess.* Asking is the only way you can positively know whether the other person does or does not want to be intimate with you.

The Body Language Challenge showed you multiple examples of how body language can cause confusion and misunderstanding between two people on a date or in a relationship. Each of the examples is a real-life scenario that frequently happens to people. Each challenge proved body language is not effective. We need to use a better form of communication.

CHAPTER 1: THE LOOK

Remember this:

- Body language is unreliable and often misinterpreted!
- To communicate effectively with your partner, utilize verbal communication.
- While on a date, do not project or force your wants onto the other person.

Try this:

Watch people in a public place. Notice the body language each person sends as they pass by other people. Now try to notice when people talk to each other. Write down the way people interact when talking is involved. Describe their expressions and animation. See whether you notice how people's expressions and emotions come alive as they talk.

Bonus

 Strictly Students: Discover two tips for correctly using body language at www.canikissyou.com/students.

 Parents Pointers: Find out what messages you are sending to your child at www.canikissyou.com/parents.

 Teachers Tool: Get three extra questions to discuss with your students at www.canikissyou.com/educators.

my**NOTES**:

2

Talking?
You Must Be Kidding

Walk up to a person and say, "Before you kiss someone, do you ask first?" How do you think the person is going to respond? First, you may hear the person laugh. You might notice the person looking at you with a "you must be kidding" look on their face. Finally, the person will probably respond with, "No way would I ask."

Why doesn't everyone ask? FEAR! Fear can be a strong factor in the choices people make. The Dating Fear Factors below are the three reasons why people do not ask first before kissing or becoming intimate with another person.

- Rejection
- Image destruction
- Humiliation

Fear of Rejection
When you avoid asking for a kiss, you are anticipating that a verbal rejection will be more humiliating than a rejection from just "making your move." You fear that hearing the word "no" would be devastating to your confidence. Could that possibly be worse than the alternative? Perhaps not to you—but what about your date's feelings?

Not asking can result in embarrassing and dangerous consequences. If you don't ask and just try your "moves" on someone, the person could push you away, slap you, turn away from you, or worse. All of these reactions are nonverbal forms of rejection.

If you just try without asking, what do you do when the other person doesn't react? If you kiss someone and they do not respond in a negative manner, you might assume the person wants you to continue. However, the person may be too uncomfortable to speak out. The person may be worried about creating a difficult situation by negatively reacting to you. In the meantime, you think everything is going great. In reality, you are creating very uncomfortable circumstances.

As you read this, did you think to yourself, "I could tell if someone did not want me to kiss them"? Have you ever known one person to return from a date talking about how awesome the date went? The person told you what a great "end of date" kiss they experienced. At the same time, the other person on the date is telling people how boring the date was and how awful the kiss at the end went. We all know this happens.

You don't ask because you fear being rejected. You just try to make your "move." Now you are rejected by being pushed away or slapped. Where is the date headed at this point? The date is probably over, and you have ruined any chance to get to know this person. Why? Because you were afraid to ask. Your fear drove you to act with disrespect for the other person's feelings. Acting in fear caused you to make another person uncomfortable. The worst result of not asking is committing a sexual assault. Asking for consent eliminates the danger and the embarrassment.

Fear of Image Destruction

You fear your image will be destroyed when everyone hears that you asked for a kiss. Some men fear looking less like a "man" or not appearing "macho." Some men fear peers calling them a "wimp." Some women fear getting a reputation for being sexually assertive. Some women fear being called "easy" and other sexually derogatory names. All individuals can fear their sexuality being questioned.

How do you get past the fear of your image being ruined? If you think the person you are dating will degrade you for asking, do not go on the date! Any time you fear what your dating partner is going to say about you, you are entering into an unhealthy and potentially hazardous dating environment.

Honor the highest standards for yourself. When going on a date, expect to be respected. Only date people who respect you. The moment you feel a lack of respect, recognize the danger and do everything you can to get out of the situation.

Fear of Humiliation

You fear looking like an idiot or a fool in front of your date. This is the number one reason people do not verbally ask before kissing or being intimate. You fear asking will make you look bad or will take away the romance of the moment.

The reason you have this negative view of asking is because you never see or hear role models ask. Consider your favorite television shows and movies. How often do you see the characters ask before they kiss? How about adults in your life? If you cannot find positive examples on television or in the movies, do not worry. These characters live in a fake world where no one gets sexually assaulted. You live in the real world. If you do feel humiliated or fear humiliating yourself, do not take it out on your date. Set the standard and be the positive example for others. Ask.

How about this?

Describe the "average" scene of intimacy you watch on television or in a movie. How do the two people approach each other? How do television shows and the movies try to make intimacy look easy and "perfect"? Think of all the differences in a "real" date versus a movie or television date. Write down all of the flaws in the "average" romantic television or movie scene.

Example

On television, Dylan enters the house. Dylan sees Jamie across the room. Music starts playing. Dylan goes toward Jamie and they just start romantically kissing. They never say anything to each other. What would happen if the typical person tried this? What would the partner think?

Roles and The Assumption Gap

When in a relationship, what roles do you tend to find yourself in? Two of the most common roles are the Passive Role and the Assertive Role. Unfortunately, in many societies, gender roles are often assigned based on a history of heterosexual relationships. Men are expected to be more assertive. Women are expected to be more passive. These stereotypes are reinforced through statements like:

- Men saying, **"Women only want the 'bad' guy."**
- Women saying, **"All guys are out for only one thing."**

These stereotypes are based on assumptions about an entire gender and reinforce negative associations about that gender. Partners assume things about each other based on historic gender roles instead of talking to each other. Thus, the perpetuation of the

Assumption Gap, the divide between the gender stereotypes of a person and who the person really is.

Are heterosexuals the only people who struggle with roles and a gap between assumptions and reality? No! People of all sexual orientations make these same mistakes. They fall into the trap of feeling a need to fulfill a "role" in the relationship. Based on one's role, the person also assumes how the partner wants to be treated romantically and/or sexually.

Do you find yourself aligning more with the Passive Role or more with the Assertive Role in an intimate relationship?

Assertive Role

The Assertive Role believes asking for a kiss is "wimpy" and would ruin the moment. The reality is that partners find asking to be very romantic. Why? A partner asking is unique. Asking makes you stand out from everyone else. Asking shows you care and only want to engage in intimacy your partner equally wants. Lastly, asking helps eliminate the Assertive Role image of "wanting only one thing."

The Assertive Role can mistake arrogance for confidence. This person will respond to the idea of asking first by stating, "Going for it without asking shows confidence. My partner can always say 'No' if they don't like what I am doing."

If you hear someone say that, stop and ask the person, "Why not ask first? You are describing a partner who is trying to stop you from doing something sexual with them that you have already begun doing. You can't reverse what you've already done to this person. Doesn't your partner deserve to have a choice before you begin engaging in sexual intimacy with their body?"

"Going for it" without asking is not a sign of confidence. It is arrogant. You are assuming you know what another person wants without asking first and finding out. Acting on that arrogance is disrespectful and dangerous, and it can be criminal.

Passive Role

There are two primary reasons the Passive Role does not take the initiative to ask for a kiss. One reason is the belief that "asking is my partner's job." The other reason is the Passive Role believes a partner would be turned off by being asked for a kiss.

Actually, many partners consider it a turn-on to be asked, especially by someone who typically is considered taking the more Passive Role. Most partners, especially in the Assertive Role, do not like having all the pressure of "knowing when to make the moves." By asking, you take all that pressure off your partner. When you ask for a kiss, your partner knows you are attracted to them and want the kiss. All of the pressure of "reading your mind" is off your partner. Often those in Assertive Roles feel stressed about making this decision. With Challenge No. 6 in Chapter 1, we showed how many hours a person may wait before making the decision to "make a move." Why? The person fears being wrong about reading the other's body language.

Believing it is "my partner's job" to be the assertive one leads to an unbalanced relationship. You are putting all the responsibility on your partner to initiate intimacy. Doing so is unfair. You are creating a one-sided relationship. By always waiting for your partner to initiate intimacy, you also appear to be giving more control over the decision to be intimate to your partner. You are surrendering a degree of power.

Never give up your self-respect! For all people to have equality, we must live by the standard of equality in every facet of our relationships. Most partners do not want the "job" of always being assigned to an assertive or passive role. If you want something, share it with your partner. Have you ever heard someone say how a partner, "expects me to read their mind; I wish my partner would just tell me"?

For too long, women and people who are not heterosexual were taught to silence their voices with regard to sexuality and relationships. Society's goal should be to empower all people to speak their minds freely. Each of us needs to do our best to continue creating equality and equal respect for everyone.

The key to eliminating the Assumption Gap is talking and listening. Ask specific questions. Eliminate assumptions. Learn what people like—not just what you assume based on a role someone may appear to be living.

People can become so concerned about how they will thrive in their roles that they fail to do what is right. Do not be controlled by a role. Be a caring person. Give your partner a choice by asking first.

How about this?

Write down questions you would like answered by someone who tends to exist in the same role as the people you find yourself most attracted to. Talk to your friends and find out what similar questions they would like to ask if given the same opportunity. Get a group of individuals of all sexual orientations and genders together to discuss the questions.

Have each person answer the questions. Do not ridicule anyone for their question or answer. Talk to each other with respect and understanding.

Mentors

Talk with people who have experienced asking or being asked for a kiss. You might have to talk to a lot of people before you find someone with experience being asked. Keep trying until you find someone. Get their honest opinion of what it felt like. You will learn how much people appreciate and enjoy being asked.

If you want to learn how to make lots of money, do you ask a person who constantly loses money? No, you ask the person who has success making lots of money. Do the same with dating. Ask the person who has experience in showing respect for their partners by asking.

CHAPTER 2: TALKING?

Remember this:

- There is no reason not to ask someone before kissing them!
- For advice, talk to people who have experienced asking.

Try this:

Get a group of friends together to play the Reverse Roles game. Have each person share whether they identify more as the Assertive or Passive Role when in a relationship (understanding that not everyone may fit into these two roles). Have a stack of small pieces of paper available for everyone to write down the stereotypes people have of each role. Put each stereotype on a separate piece of paper. Separate the stereotypes into two piles: Passive and Assertive.

Each team randomly picks a piece of paper from the pile of their role's stereotypes. The team then explains why their role is known for that stereotype. The other team can counter with ways the stereotype could be eliminated. This game can be very silly, lots of fun, and really get everyone thinking.

Example:

The Assertive Team picks up a piece of paper that the Passive Team wrote about the Assertive Role. The paper says, "Assertives try to be macho on dates." The Assertive Team explains why they do this or why the Passive Team may be misinterpreting what Assertives do, and then the Passive Team shares why they dislike Assertives doing that. You can have lots of people laughing and learning! Now the challenge is for the Passive Team to give examples of what they would like instead.

Bonus

 Strictly Students: Find out how you may be discriminating at www.canikissyou.com/students.

 Parents' Pointers: Get the secret to creating equality for your son or daughter in relationships at www.canikissyou.com/parents.

 Teachers' Tool: Discover how to encourage all genders to speak out at www.canikissyou.com/educators.

my**NOTES**:

3

The Time Is Now
Do You Know How?

At this point, you know that body language is not reliable. You have eliminated all reasons for not asking. You have no excuses for not showing the highest level of respect for your dating partner by asking before you try kissing.

So what is the last hurdle? Inexperience. Trying something you have never seen done is difficult. At first, asking may seem challenging, but remember, as long as you ask in a respectful manner, there is no "wrong" way to ask for a kiss.

The key to asking is keeping one thought in the forefront of your mind: Why you are asking? You are asking because you do not want to make the other person feel uncomfortable. You are asking because you do not want to do something to another person you will regret. Once you touch someone, you can't act like it didn't happen. You are asking because you care for and respect the person you are with. For these reasons, you will ask with a caring and respectful approach.

Is asking romantic? This is a common question people have. Being romantic is treating your date with compassion, respect, and care. Asking is the ultimate sign of romance. People of all genders are attracted to people who ask. Examine the two scenarios below. As you read the "Passive Asks" and the "Assertive Asks" sections (referencing Chapter 2), choose whether you think most people would respond with Option No. 1 or Option No. 2.

PASSIVE and ASSERTIVE

Throughout the rest of the book, you will notice that I refer to Passive and Assertive as examples of characters and/or individuals in given situations. Too many books depend on heteronormative language, especially referring only to heterosexual couples in their examples. I made that same mistake early in my writing. I have not assigned gender to either descriptor in this book.

Throughout the book, choose which role and/or character best describes you in each scenario being discussed. You may notice that you fit different roles depending on the situation being described.

PASSIVE ROLE ASKS

Two people, Hunter (Passive) and Peyton (Assertive), are alone at the end of a date. The night is going really well. Hunter turns to Peyton and says, "I have a question I really want to ask you." Peyton asks, "What is it?" Hunter asks, "Can I kiss you?" Assuming Peyton wanted to be kissed, how do you think Peyton will react to being asked?

Option No. 1: Peyton says, "I can't believe you just asked. I am supposed to be the one to ask and to make the first move. Now you ruined it for me."

Option No. 2: A smile quickly comes across Peyton's face as Peyton says, "Yes!"

ASSERTIVE ROLE ASKS

Peyton (Assertive) and Hunter (Passive) are alone at the end of a date. The night is going really well. Peyton turns to Hunter and says, "I have a question I really want to ask you." Hunter asks, "What is it?" Peyton stumbles over the words to say, looks Hunter in the eyes, and then asks, "Can I kiss you?" Assuming Hunter wants to be kissed, how will Hunter react to being asked?

Option No. 1: Hunter says, "What are you doing asking? If you ask, something is wrong with you. You should have just gone for it."

Option No. 2: Hunter smiles in pleasant surprise and answers, "Yes!"

Which option did you pick in the "Assertive Role Asks" and "Passive Role Asks"? Most people will pick Option No. 2 for both scenes. Assuming both people want to kiss, how could anyone truly be "turned off" by being asked? The examples above show how foolish the concept "asking is not romantic" sounds. If a friend tells you, "Asking will ruin the moment," present both options from above. Help your friend realize how this statement lacks common sense.

 How about this?

What if you did ask someone and the person answered with the responses from Option No. 1? What would you do? This is the perfect time to open up conversation between the two of you. Learn why the person has these beliefs of certain "roles" with intimacy. The person may not understand the need for someone to show respect toward a date.

Discuss this person's views of dating. Be understanding. Write down every answer you think of. Discuss your answers with friends to decide which approach is both reasonable and respectful.

Ask yourself, "When I ask for a kiss, which person would I prefer to ask? The person who responded with Option No. 1 or the person who responded with Option No. 2?" Hopefully you are going to pick the person in Option No. 2. Why? The person appears to be considerate, appreciative, and respectful.

Did you catch a potential problem with the previous two examples? The earlier dialogues discuss two people who want to kiss each other. Does this always happen? No. How do you handle being turned down?

Rejection—You Choose!

Do you remember how you can be rejected if you don't ask and you just "make a move"? Getting slapped, hit, pushed away, or given the cold shoulder are just a few forms of the physical rejection you can experience. Once you are physically rejected by someone, in what direction is the date going? In a downward spiral!

When you ask for a kiss, what is the most likely form of getting turned down? Hearing the word "No" and then hearing a reason. The reasons could vary from "I don't kiss on the first date" to "I don't think now is the right time" or "I am not comfortable enough with our relationship."

Reacting to being turned down is the tough part. You asked because you wanted to show total respect for the other person. Now, he or she has turned you down. What do you say? What do you do? Is this date doomed?

Let the person know why you asked. In a caring and relieved voice, say, "Then I am glad I asked, because the last thing I would want to do is make you feel uncomfortable." Across the country, the reactions to this sentence range from a heartfelt "Awww" to others saying, "Wow! Smooth." All genders and sexual orientations have an amazingly positive reaction. Why?

Are you using a "line" on the person? No. A "line" is a made up or contrived comment to try to impress the other person. Most "lines" fail miserably. Why is this comment not a line? Because telling someone, "Then I am glad I asked, because the last thing I would want to do is make you feel uncomfortable" is the real reason you are asking. You are asking because you don't want to make the other person uncomfortable. By making this statement, all you are doing is telling the TRUTH!

After sharing the truth, where is the date going? Is the date ruined or spiraling downward? No. Can you still make this date a success? Yes. In fact, the relationship between the two of you may be stronger after this experience because you have respected each other's boundaries. You have created a level of equal respect between the two of you.

Here are two examples of how a partner can react to being asked first, answering "No," and having you respect the answer.

Partner "A," who said "No" to a kiss, responds by saying, "I never expected the person to ask, especially the way they handled my saying 'No.' By accepting my not wanting to kiss at that moment, the person showed me that they are not just on this date to 'get something' from me. This person appears to care about me. This makes me want to get to know the person better."

Partner "B," who said "No" to a kiss, responds by saying, "Wow! The way the date was going, I just felt no connection between the two of us and didn't feel like kissing. When the person asked me for a kiss, I was really worried about how my saying 'No' would go. The person was so cool about it. I found it easy for us to talk during the rest of the date."

Being honest and open with each other can lead to more meaningful discussions. Imagine if everyone were honest on dates. You could learn whether the two of you were dating each other for the same reasons. You could learn whether the person had different intentions than you. You could stop a bad or dangerous date before it ever began.

How about this?

Write down several "wrong" reasons for someone to date you. Each person can have very different answers to this question. Next, write the reasons you want a person to date you.

Example

I don't want to date someone who is focused on how much money I have. I want someone to date me because they enjoy my sense of humor.

Two of the common concerns with asking for intimacy are below:

Asking for Intimacy Concern No. 1: "It is only a kiss. What is the big deal if you kiss someone and they don't want it?"

The kiss is the beginning of intimacy. The standard you establish in the beginning sets the tone for the rest of the relationship.

Establishing, expressing, and honoring boundaries sets a high standard of respect right from the start.

Asking for Intimacy Concern No. 2: "Talking about 'doing something' with someone is too difficult. Just trying it with each other is much easier."

Doesn't the above comment lack common sense? If you are not comfortable talking about an act of intimacy with your partner, why are you engaging in the intimacy? When you realize you cannot talk to someone about a certain level of intimacy, you are not ready to engage in that level of intimacy. The golden rule of dating is: *If you can't talk about It, don't do It!*

 How about this?

Get a group of friends together. Role play the scene of asking for a kiss or an intimate act. First, have the person ask by trying to use a typical "line" with the partner. Next, have the person ask in a caring and straightforward fashion. Have the partner answer "No" in one example and "Yes" in the other example.

The role play is a role play. Neither person should ever touch the other person or actually try to kiss the other person.

Now, reverse roles! Have the partner ask both ways. Have the person being asked answer "No" once and "Yes" the second time. How can you change the scenario one more time and try it again? After each attempt at asking, talk with everyone about what it looked like, sounded like, and felt like. When trying something for the first time, the best approach is practice, practice, and practice. By role-playing with friends, you can practice without the threat of facing real rejection or embarrassment.

What about more than a kiss? "Okay, I will definitely ask before I kiss someone, but what about more than a kiss? How do I ask someone if I can do specific intimate acts with them? Won't I take away the excitement?"

Being able to talk about sexual intimacy is a sign of maturity and responsibility. By talking, each of you learns what acts of intimacy the other person enjoys doing the most and wants to do together. With this knowledge, you are more equipped to please each other.

Robin, Loren's married partner, comes home and says, "Loren, tonight I am going to put the kids to bed by 8:00 p.m., and then I want you to meet me in bed for some fun." If Loren wants to engage in sexual intimacy with Robin that night, which of the following two responses is Loren more likely to give? "I don't like it when we plan our intimacy or talk about it. No thanks." Or "Yes. I can't wait till 8:00 p.m."

As silly as this example may sound, everyone agrees Loren is much more likely to be excited about 8:00 p.m. When you talk, the intimacy is more exciting because you look forward to experiencing the intimate acts you both enjoy the most. Talking greatly improves intimacy.

IMPORTANT: Being intimate with a person can involve tremendous risks. No form of "100 percent safe sex" exists. If you decide to be intimately involved with another person, seek professional guidance on how to protect yourself and your partner from sexually transmitted infections and/or unintended pregnancy. Please be as safe as possible in your decisions.

Ask yourself, "Why am I choosing to engage in this activity with this person?" If the answer is "for fun" or "because I really like this person," remind yourself of all the risks and the potential impact on both your futures. If you choose not to engage in the sexual activity, a partner who has respect for you will honor your choice. Respect yourself at all times.

Values List

Holding yourself to high standards is easier when you believe in yourself and your values. On a scale of 1 to 10, write down how you would score yourself as a person. Ten is the highest score and one is the lowest score. Ten is not perfect. Being a "10" simply means you believe you are the best person you can be.

You can be a 10. Did you score yourself a 10? If you didn't score yourself a 10, do it now. Write a list of what makes you a 10. Write down every aspect of who you are that makes you unique, special, and valuable. Then write a list with all of your personal values.

Get together with friends and review each person's list. While listening to your friends' lists, you will think of values you forgot about but that you know you believe in. Add those values to your list.

After each person reads their list, encourage the group to tell that person more items that can be added. Often friends see strengths and values in you that you don't notice. Now you have a large list of values. Cherish this list. When you wake up each morning, read it out loud. (No one else has to hear you.) Reading the list out loud will help tell your brain to honor these values and reinforce your image of self-respect.

Examples of personal values can include:

- **"I do the right thing."**
- **"I have compassion for others."**
- **"I respect all people."**
- **"My body is precious."**

At the end of each day, ask yourself, "Did the actions I took and decisions I made today fit the values I believe in? Did today's actions and decisions add to my value?"

 How about this?

Recall a time when you took an action or made a decision against your values; then decide why you made the negative choice. Write down the reason and how it resulted in a negative outcome. Did it make you feel bad? Did it make someone else feel bad? Would you do the same today? By noticing mistakes, you have the ability to steer away from a future negative choice.

Now recall a decision that added to your value; write it down. Write down why you made the choice and how that choice made you feel. Remind yourself how rewarding making a positive decision feels.

Get together with your friends and share your experiences. From school to dating, help each other stay away from bad choices. Applaud each other for making good choices. By sharing your decisions, your friends can help hold you accountable to your commitment of living with high standards and values.

> **IMPORTANT: If you make a choice against your values or standards and then someone harms you, know the person who did the harm is the person responsible for the harm. Not you.**

Example, Phoenix is on a first date that is going amazingly. The two of them begin kissing and later agree to sexually touching each other. Even though sexual touching goes against Phoenix's standards on a first date, Phoenix feels this moment is right. Suddenly, Phoenix's partner says, "We've gone this far. You have to go all the way." Phoenix doesn't want to "go all the way" and yet the partner continues doing so against Phoenix's will. Regardless of whether Phoenix made a previous choice against Phoenix's values (such as sexually touching a partner on a first date), Phoenix is not responsible for the partner forcing the unwanted sexual activity. The partner is the one responsible for doing the harm.

What does creating a Values List have to do with healthy dating and relationships? When you possess positive values, people will be less likely to affect your decision-making process in a negative way. When you have values based on respect, you will not take actions to hurt another person. When you believe in your values, a date will be less likely to succeed in persuading you to partake in actions you are not comfortable with. You will speak more freely about your opinions and beliefs. You will project an image of strength and respect.

The healthiest relationships are built on respect: Respect for yourself, respect for your partner, and respect through open and honest communication. Exercise respect for yourself and your partner by talking with each other. Remember the golden rule of intimacy: **If you can't talk about it, don't do it.**

CHAPTER 3: THE TIME IS NOW

Remember this:

- Ask with respect. Respect the answer.
- Asking is the ultimate sign of romance!
- Tell the person why you asked.
- Create open and honest conversations.
- Believe in your values. Add to your values.
- Don't try it if you can't talk about it!

Try this:

Write a script for two people on a date. Create fun and respectful dialogue that reinforces the strength in talking and asking. Donate the script to a local school for its health classes to use as a role-playing scene between students.

Bonus

 Strictly Students: Read the biggest fear that keeps many people from asking at www.canikissyou.com/students.

 Parents' Pointers: Take the "Respect Survey" for your family at www.canikissyou.com/parents.

 Teachers' Tool: Get the "What If" exercise at www.canikissyou.com/educators.

my**NOTES**:

4

Do I Have to Ask?
Why?

Could you sexually assault another person? While most people answer "No," many of these same people have already committed a sexual assault. Did you know a sexual assault can occur on the average date when a couple becomes sexually intimate for the first time? How can this be?

Let's start with the meaning of sexual assault as discussed in this book. The legal definition and the prosecution of sexual assault vary by state. Consequently, this book is not referring to any specific legal standard. To learn more about the laws, visit the Resources section at www.DateSafeProject.org. Throughout the book, I am referring to a definition of sexual assault that reflects an ideal such that if everyone agreed to live in a manner that didn't violate this definition, no one would experience any form of sexual activity without consent. Thus, in this book, sexual assault is referred to as:

Sexual contact without consent for the purpose of sexual gratification and/or degradation.

Like with other crimes, sexual assault can have varying degrees (first degree, second degree, third degree, and fourth degree) and they can vary by state. The lowest degree may be sexual contact without consent. Sexual intercourse without consent would be a higher degree of sexual assault.

Why the wording "for the purpose of sexual gratification and/ or degradation"? This definition allows for the possibility that sexual contact can occur that is not intentional. Example: a person is at a crowded party. As the person turns around to talk to a friend, the person accidentally brushes up against a woman's breast or a man's genitalia. The person was not trying to make sexual contact for the purpose of sexual gratification or degradation. This example would not be a sexual assault.

Consent is a key component to defining sexual assault. Briefly write down what the word "consent" means to you. If you want consent to borrow something from another person, what do you do? You ask.

Understanding consent is essential to healthy relationships and sexual intimacy. Years ago, consent was synonymous with "permission," which is not a good way to define consent. You might be able to get someone's permission to engage in a sexual act the person does not want to participate in. What is a better definition of consent?

Consent is a freely given and mutually wanted enthusiastic agreement between partners of sound mind and legal age.

Sounds wonderful, right? Sexual intimacy should be wonderful and wanted by all partners.

Do people ask before they kiss or touch someone in an intimate area? Not usually! We know people assume consent by trying to read body language—body language, which we have learned, is unreliable. Since most people do not receive consent, they are acting under the parameters of a sexual assault. Thus, a sexual assault is likely to happen on a date where a couple is becoming intimate for the first time.

To help discover the need for changes in the way we approach intimacy, read the following paragraph. Ask yourself whether this example could reflect a typical date. Ask yourself whether you know people who have been on this type of a date.

Two of your friends, Logan and Kai, are going on a date together for the first time. Logan asks Kai out because Logan is attracted to Kai. As the date advances, Logan feels comfortable with Kai. Logan thinks Kai wants to be intimate. At this point, Logan tries to kiss Kai. Immediately, Logan thinks Kai wants the kiss, and so continues. Over time, Logan touches Kai more intimately. Logan continues advancing the touching until Kai stops Logan. Logan stops.

Where is the sexual assault? Think about when Logan stopped. Logan only stopped when Kai took action to stop Logan. Logan had already been touching Kai without asking first.

How uncomfortable would most people be before they took physical or strong verbal action to stop a partner? Across the country, I ask audiences this very question. The average person says they will not normally take action to stop a partner unless they are very uncomfortable with the actions taking place or the partner is already doing something not wanted. By the point the person is trying to stop the partner, the partner has gone too far (just like the example with Logan and Kai). A sexual assault has already taken place.

Perpetrators of sexual assault try to argue that the other person gave "implied" consent because they did not do anything to stop the assailant earlier in the date. If you don't say anything or take any action against the assailant, are you giving consent? No! As we have learned, receiving consent means getting someone's agreement to participate in the sexual intimacy. Agreement requires a response. If you did not respond, you have not given agreement nor permission.

Try using "implied" consent as an excuse for robbery. You are walking down the street and I approach you. As I get near you, I pull a gun out and tell you to give me all your money. You freeze. You don't say anything. I take your money and run off. However, I get caught and go to trial for robbery.

In this robbery case, my defense attorney is going to argue you gave "implied consent" for me to take your money. How? You didn't tell me "not to take your money" or to stop robbing you. You must have wanted me to take your money. Does this defense of "implied consent" sound ridiculous? Yes. Sadly, some sexual assault assailants have successfully used a similar defense of "implied consent" against their victims.

On the date we mentioned earlier, why didn't your friend, Kai, speak up or stop Logan sooner? This question is repeatedly asked by society. What is the inherent problem with this question? The question implies it was Kai's responsibility to stop Logan's actions. Who took the action?

From the scenario you read, Logan took the action. When you choose to assert yourself upon another person, who is responsible for your actions? You are! Therefore, Logan was responsible. You cannot blame Kai for Logan's actions.

When did Logan get consent? Logan didn't. Logan never knew that Kai definitely wanted any of the intimate actions Logan took. Logan couldn't know because Logan didn't ask. You should never blame the survivor for the assailant's actions.

Was Logan a horrible person? No. Sexual assault is often not about a bad person or scary strangers. Sexual assault is more routinely about the average couple. Sexual assault can happen when good people are engaged in sexual intimacy with each other and one person acts with disregard for the other person's feelings and rights.

Does the aggressor always intentionally hurt the victim? Not necessarily, but that factor doesn't matter. If you hurt someone, your ignorance or your intentions do not erase or decrease the survivor's pain and trauma. To avoid this kind of escalation, it is necessary to check in and ask your partner for consent before being intimate.

While we are discussing a situation where people might be expecting some form of sexual intimacy with each other, sexual assault does also occur between two people who know each other very well, trust each other, and one of the two does not expect any form of sexual intimacy to occur. Suddenly, one partner forces sexual activity on the other person. Please know that friends can be capable of sexually assaulting people they appear to care about and have built a trusting relationship with.

Whom do you center your thoughts on at a moment when you want to initiate sexual intimacy? If you think, "Do I have to ask?" you are thinking of yourself first. "Do I have to?" sounds like someone having to clean their room or mow the lawn. You appear to be annoyed by having to ask. In the case of dating or sexual intimacy, you are talking about the respect of another person's mind and body—not a minor issue of annoyance.

When you think, "My partner deserves to have a choice, and therefore, I need to ask," you are defining your dating partner as a person of value—an equal to yourself. Comprehending and believing in the need to ask is essential. Out of respect for the person, you need to ask. The best thought process is, "I want to ask." "I want to ask" is a positive statement and will leave a stronger impression in your mind.

Respect and the Law

What is your mental focus on a date? Focusing strictly on the law is not the best way to approach a date. When individuals consider the law, many regularly think, "I won't get caught" or "How can I get around the law?" Should you learn the law in your state? Yes. Once you know and understand the law, focus on respect. If you act with the utmost respect for your dating partner and for yourself, you will not need to concentrate only on the law. Consider the harm to others, not just the risk to yourself.

On a date or in a relationship, disregard for the law is likely to result in disrespecting your partner. If you think, "How can I get around asking to be intimate?" you are taking the risk of hurting the other person. Hurting another person or making a person uncomfortable is not a risk to take on a date. **Dating with respect is much more fun and is safer for everyone.**

Wanting to act respectfully will inspire you to ask before becoming more intimately involved. Respect is the key to safer and healthier relationships.

What is the definition of RESPECT? On Dictionary.com, respect is defined as: *to hold in esteem or honor; to show regard or consideration for; to refrain from intruding upon or interfering with; to relate or have reference to.*

The combination of all four of the above definitions is vital to the definition of respect in relationships and sexual intimacy. You should treat each person with esteem and honor. You should show regard and consideration for your partner's wants, wishes, and boundaries.

You should refrain from intruding upon or interfering with your partner's wants, wishes, and boundaries. You should relate to and show deference to your partner's feelings and boundaries. Likewise, you deserve to have all four of these elements of respect given to you!

For the partner who says, "I touched your butt without asking because it was so fine. I was completely giving you respect. I was honoring your fine behind," clearly the person was not refraining from intruding upon your wants and/or boundaries. Consequently, this person was not respecting you or your boundaries.

Live with respect for yourself and your partner.

Long-Term Relationships

After you have asked a person for the first kiss, do you need to continue to ask for further intimacy? Yes. Each person can have a different comfort level with intimacy. To learn each other's boundaries, talk to each other. The process of talking to each other helps create a comfort level between both people and a stronger foundation for future intimacy.

If you are married, do you still need consent? Yes. Married partners can, and have, sexually assaulted their partners. Whether you have been dating for three months or have been married for forty years, no person owes sexual or intimate acts to a partner. It is not a boyfriend's, a girlfriend's, a wife's, a husband's, or a partner's job to be sexually active with a partner. People in long-term relationships and marriages still need consent. Talk with each other to ensure that each person wants the intimacy. Regardless of how long the relationship has existed, mutual respect is essential in all relationships.

 How about this?

What are challenges that couples in long-term relationships

face with communicating, talking, and getting consent? Analyze each of your answers and find a solution that emphasizes respect. Try role-playing each challenge and solution.

Example

Once they have been intimate together, one of the people assumes intimacy is their right whenever they want it. You could explain that each act of intimacy is separate from the last act. In all cases, both people need to "want" the intimacy. While statistically and historically, men are more often perpetrators of sexual assault, all genders are capable of committing a sexual assault. There is no standard profile of a sexual assault assailant.

 How about this?

Could you sexually assault another person? What actions will you take to ensure you never commit a sexual assault? Write down what you are going to do differently to ensure that you respect yourself and your partner and will never commit a sexual assault.

When you complete the list, read your answers out loud. Why write down your answers and then read the answers out loud? The brain more effectively retains information presented to it in various formats—reading, writing, and speaking.

Once you feel comfortable with making your statements out loud, share your ideas with other people. Your actions to stop sexual assaults from happening will help protect people from becoming victims of sexual assault.

CHAPTER 4: DO I HAVE TO ASK?

Remember this:

- Sexual Assault = Sexual Contact without Consent!
- Consent is needed for every action. Always ask!
- Be responsible for your actions.
- Think, "I want to ask."

Try this:

Create two sets of posters. In the first set, teach people how sexual assault affects everyone. In the second set, show people how respecting their dates results in fun and healthy relationships. Be creative. Get permission to place the posters in local schools or colleges.

Bonus

 Strictly Students: Read about how to talk about consent at www.canikissyou.com/students.

 Parents' Pointers: Learn how to talk to your child about healthy relationships at www.canikissyou.com/parents.

 Teachers' Tool: Discover a way to teach "ongoing consent" to your students at www.canikissyou.com/educators.

my**NOTES**:

5

You Don't Have to Know
And You Can Still Help

D o you know the pain and trauma caused by a sexual assault? The emotional pain can be unthinkable. Understanding the trauma of a sexual assault can help each of us see the need to change the current "status quo" of relationships and sexual intimacy. Sexual assault is considered to be the most devastating crime a person can survive.

While we know that any individual can be sexually assaulted, gender can affect the realities of sexual assault. Statistically, women are more likely to experience being sexually assaulted. Given this reality, when a woman dates, she may be thinking about the potential danger her partner presents to her, especially if the partner is physically stronger. The partner's physical being can be a weapon used against her. In addition to the partner's body being a weapon, sex and sex acts are weapons the perpetrator might use against her.

When previously comparing robbery to sexual assault, we showed why the comparison is not fair to an assault survivor. Some people would say the comparison is not fair because the thief possessed a gun, which creates a more severe threat of danger. However, the sexual perpetrator on a date possesses the weapon of potentially forcing one's body and sexual acts onto another person against that person's will. The perpetrator could, with their own body or with an object, violently penetrate the most private parts of another person's body.

Historically, many heterosexual men do not believe there is a possibility they could be sexually assaulted. They do not believe a dating or sexual partner could ever overpower them. Not relating to the fear of being sexually assaulted may cause heterosexual men to have difficulty relating to the trauma of sexual assault and limit seeking support after an assault.

For years, educational programs would use the example of a man-on-man sexual assault to help men connect with the horror of the crime of sexual assault. When they would tell a heterosexual guy to imagine a man raping a man, he would often cringe as he would say, "Disgusting." You would hear men and women respond to a man-on-man sexual assault with statements such as, "That is gross because a man raping a man is not natural. I mean, you are talking about two guys." Are these people trying to say a woman being sexually assaulted by a man is natural? No act of sexual assault should be considered natural or more acceptable!

Sadly, these reactions are rooted in homophobia. For this reason, we do not recommend using those examples to help someone better relate to the pain caused by sexual assault. People of all genders and sexual orientations deserve equal dignity, compassion, and respect.

In recent years, more people in our society are learning about sexual assault and beginning to understand how horrific sexual assault is for all survivors.

Comprehending the pain and suffering caused by sexual assault helps us understand how horrific and unnatural this crime is. As I have traveled the country, I have met thousands of sexual assault survivors. I can share with you the anguish I have seen and experienced in talking with survivors, but I cannot tell you what it is like to be sexually assaulted.

 How about this?

How can you learn more about the trauma a sexual assault survivor experiences? Contact a local rape crisis center or your state coalition against sexual assault. Find out the next time a program is being presented by a sexual assault survivor. Attend the program. Listen closely to the lessons the survivor will share with you. If you are in school, work with your school to invite a survivor to come and speak.

Survivors will tell you how being sexually assaulted can destroy your ability to feel safe. In almost every case, the assailant is a person the survivor knows. What if your assailant lives near you or goes to the same school you attend? Imagine going to class and having to sit in the same room as the person who sexually assaulted you. Survivors often want to drop out of school or transfer because of the fear of being near their assailants.

Before being assaulted, you take for granted going out and having fun. After being assaulted, you might look at every person and wonder whether you are safe. If someone you know can hurt you so badly, what might other people do to you? How can you trust anyone?

Thoughts of being intimate and having healthy sexual relations are usually very positive thoughts. Once you have been assaulted, your mind can have a very different view. You can be scared and frightened of what might happen during a moment of sexual intimacy. You question if the person you are with could also behave like the assailant who sexually assaulted you.

If you knew your assailant, your mind hasn't forgotten the trust you might have put in the person. Due to this memory, your mind can find it very difficult to trust anyone in any intimate situation. Why does the mind not forget? Your mind is very powerful and wants to protect you from any potential harm. By keeping the negative images in front of you, your mind is trying to remind you of what could happen to you.

HELP!

Professional counseling for sexual assault survivors can be extremely helpful. Working with a professional counselor can help bring meaningful and lifesaving results to a survivor. Without an outlet for survivors to discuss their trauma and emotions, their feelings are likely to build up inside of them. The stress from the buildup can be both mentally and physically damaging to the survivor.

Survivors may also be in future situations where they may be triggered as a result of the assault. Triggering is when something occurs that results in the survivor being reminded of the past sexual assault. Triggers can lead to sudden and unexpected reactions that can impact all five senses and can cause severe distress and pain. Seeking professional help for processing the assault is important.

Working with a professional can help a survivor move forward to lead a healthy and wonderful life. *I use the term "survivor" because the person has survived. Survivors are strong and courageous individuals. Some survivors do not recognize the strength and courage inside of themselves yet.* The more you can reinforce the understanding that survivors are incredible people, the more you can help each survivor see the positive possibilities ahead of them.

Unfortunately, most survivors never get professional help. Survivors do not seek out help for two main reasons:

1. False stigma associated with counseling

When thinking of getting help through a counselor, people sometimes have a reaction of, "I am not sick or crazy. I do not need a counselor." Seeing a counselor does not mean you are sick, crazy, or less of a person. Counseling is an outstanding resource for survivors. Being willing to seek professional support can be a sign of strength and courage.

A counselor is like a coach. Why does every great athlete in the world have a coach? The coach can tell athletes components of their game that the athletes cannot see while they are playing. A counselor can help you see what is happening in your life. A counselor can help you deal with your emotions and thoughts. A counselor can help improve your life and aid in your healing process.

2. Privacy

Survivors may fear what they say to a counselor could be used against them or reported to the authorities. Young survivors fear their parents will be notified or their peers will find out.

Rape crisis centers have been created across the continent to solve these concerns for survivors. Rape crisis centers provide confidential counseling to survivors. You can call a center and talk to a professional without fear of your privacy being violated.

Can privacy laws change? Yes. If you are not sure of the law in your state, just ask. When you call a rape crisis center, ask the professional if your conversations are confidential. The laws can be different for minors and adults. If you are under age eighteen, tell the person that you are a minor to ensure that the professional is giving you the correct legal information for your situation.

To find the rape crisis center closest to you or for immediate support available 24 hours a day, call R.A.I.N.N.'s hotline at 800-656-HOPE (4673). R.A.I.N.N. is the Rape, Abuse, & Incest National Network.

Many college campuses provide their own counseling services at the campus health center. Military installations have Sexual Assault Response Coordinators (SARCs) and Victim Advocates. Aircraft Carriers are now staffed with Deployed Resiliency Counselors.

In addition to rape crisis centers, you can look up rape crisis lines, such as R.A.I.N.N. provides at 800-656-HOPE (4673), which are phone services staffed with trained personnel to help rape survivors through their trauma. If the survivor was recently assaulted, this is a great starting point. An assault is an unbelievably emotional and stressful time for the survivor. Whether an assault occurred years ago or minutes ago, *let the professionals help*. Call a rape crisis line, such as R.A.I.N.N., or a rape crisis center. The services are often provided by the same agency.

Seeking medical treatment after a sexual assault can be critical to the life of the survivor. An assault can expose a survivor to pregnancy, infections, and sexually transmitted infections. Medical professionals can help manage these risks. The Violence Against Women Act (VAWA) of 2013 gives all victims of sexual assault the right to a medical forensic examination without reporting to law enforcement or participating in a criminal justice investigation (to learn more about VAWA, visit www.evawintl.org). If the survivor decides to report the assault to law enforcement at a later time, the physical evidence and the documentation of the assault by a forensic examiner can be vital to the criminal case. Medical forensic examinations and evidence collection is usually offered twenty-four hours a day whether in emergency rooms or free standing facilities.

If you have a friend who is a survivor of sexual assault, do you force the survivor into counseling or into reporting the crime? No. Your friend's perpetrator already forced your friend into something they did not want to do. The last thing you want to do to a friend is to take power and control away from them. Highly encourage your friend to get counseling and to report the crime. Provide the proper information so your friend can take control and make their own informed decisions.

If the survivor is hesitant, encourage them to call a rape crisis line to talk with a professional. Explain the benefits of talking with a professional. Let the survivor know they deserve to talk with a supportive professional. Offer to go with your friend to a counseling center and to the authorities. Never force counseling. Never force your friend to file a criminal report. Always respect the survivor's choices.

How about this?

Go on the Internet and do research under rape crisis centers, crisis lines, state coalitions against sexual assault, and national organizations working to support survivors. A great place to start is at www.DateSafeProject.org in the "Resources" section where you'll find lots of links to helpful agencies and organizations. Visit as many of these sites as possible and collect specific information on how their services can help a survivor. With this knowledge, you will be better prepared to help a survivor.

Blaming the Survivor

Would you know if a friend or family member was the survivor of a sexual assault? No, not normally. Most survivors do not talk openly about their assaults—not even to close family and friends. The reason for this secrecy is because our society has a history of treating sexual assault survivors poorly.

You can find numerous examples of survivors being blamed for being sexually assaulted. The comments below are just a few statements survivors have heard people say. Each statement is followed by reasons why the comment is wrong:

"The person asked for it."
Impossible. You cannot ask to be assaulted. An assault occurs without consent!

"That is what happens when you act like a tease."
You have the right to set your own personal standards on how far you feel comfortable engaging in sexual activity with another person. You always deserve to have your standards respected.

"You can't be getting it on with someone and then stop."
You always have the right to stop. If you say, "Yes" and then change your mind, you have the right to stop in the middle of whatever you are doing.

When an assault takes place, the assailant is at fault. The assailant took the action, not the survivor. Our society does not blame the victim of other crimes such as robbery, burglary, and auto theft. For example, you don't hear anyone state that a person shouldn't have been wearing a nice watch or driving a cool car. We have no excuses for blaming the survivor of a sexual assault.

Imagine being sexually assaulted and then hearing someone blame you for the assault. Imagine if the person blaming you was a family member or a friend. Would you want to continue talking about the assault? Blaming the survivor is a major cause of survivors not speaking out about their assaults and not reporting the assaults to the authorities.

 How about this?

In schools and on college campuses, how do students react to hearing about a sexual assault? Do they blame the assailant or the survivor? Try to think of reasons people try to blame a survivor. Then find the fault in the reasoning. As we have learned, a survivor doesn't ask to be sexually assaulted and should never be blamed.

Example

What if the assailant is popular and well-liked? Whom will people support and whom will they blame? People might blame the survivor because they don't want to believe a "good" person could assault someone.

Supporting Survivors

How have you reacted when you heard about a sexual assault case? From the comments that you made, will a survivor think you are going to be supportive? Starting today, say the right words. Talk to everyone you care about and share the following message (referred to as "Opening the Door" for survivors):

"If anyone ever has or ever does sexually touch you against your will or without your consent, I am always here for you. Always."

Avoid adding statements such as, "If anyone ever does anything to you, I'll kill the person." Comments of retaliation or violence will often scare the survivor and keep them from telling anyone what happened. Focus the conversation solely on supporting the survivor.

Why is it important to begin to tell everyone you can within the next few hours and days? You never know when someone has been or will be sexually assaulted. If a person hears you "Opening the Door" and is sexually assaulted months later, the survivor is likely to remember that you are a safe outlet. Or, if the person had been sexually assaulted in the past, they may see you as the one person who will be helpful and understanding.

Now that you have opened the door for a survivor, what do you say when someone tells you they were sexually assaulted? Many people mistakenly respond by saying, "I'm sorry," which survivors frequently feel is a statement of pity. Instead, show respect and admiration for the survivor by saying:

"Thank you for sharing with me. Clearly, you are strong and courageous. What can I do to help?"

Let the survivor decide what to discuss. Listen closely. From earlier in this chapter, you know the many options available to survivors. When appropriate, share those options. When "Opening the Door" for a survivor, you have the opportunity to make a positive impact on the life of another person.

Changing through Engaging

Do you know how to help change society's approach to supporting survivors of sexual assault? Do you notice how people negatively talk about what the survivor "did" in a sexual assault case? Any time you hear a person acting in a disrespectful manner to a survivor, approach that person. Engage the person in conversation. Do not attack the person for their comments. When verbally attacked, people attack back. You want to open the person's mind, not close it. Ask the person why they have the beliefs they are expressing. After listening, help them understand the fault in their reasoning. Under no circumstances is a survivor at fault for being sexually assaulted.

Taking the time to educate one person can change the lives of many!

CHAPTER 5: YOU DON'T HAVE TO KNOW

Remember this:

- Sexual assault is unnatural.
- Sexual assault is traumatic.
- Sexual assault impacts all genders and sexual orientations.
- Only the assailant should be blamed for the assault.
- Start "Opening the Door" for family and friends.
- Respect a survivor's choices.
- Counseling can aid in a survivor's healing.
- All victims of sexual assault have the right to a free medical examination.
- Survivors can speak confidentially to rape crisis centers' staff.
- Take time to educate others.

Try this:

Donate your time to a local rape crisis center.

Bonus

 Strictly Students: The "3 in 3 Rule." Get it at www.canikissyou.com/students.

 Parents' Pointers: Learn why it is essential for your teenager to have a Strong Sexual Standard at www.canikissyou.com/parents.

 Teachers' Tool: The "Blame Game" is at www.canikissyou.com/educators.

my**NOTES**:

6

Do You Understand?
The Crime, The Effect

o you understand sexual assault? Do you comprehend the various forms of sexual assault? Sexual assault is a crime of power, of one person forcing their wants onto another person, whether it be through physical violence or through mental or emotional manipulation.

> For example, Chris and Reese are being intimate with each other. Chris asks Reese whether Reese wants to have sex. Reese says, "No." Chris continues to try to persuade Reese into having sex. Reese says, "No." Chris goes back to kissing for a little while. Chris comes back to asking Reese whether Reese wants to have sex. Reese says, "No." Now Reese is getting scared. After continually telling Chris "No," Chris is not giving up. Reese is starting to worry about what Chris might do to Reese if Reese keeps saying "No." Chris asks again. This time, Chris is pushing the issue even more strongly. Out of fear that Chris will become physically violent, Reese says, "Yes."

Reese did not want to have sex with Chris. Did Reese give consent? No. Consent cannot be given under duress or a perceived threat of harm.

Did Chris put Reese in a state of being under duress or in a perceived threat of harm? Yes. Chris's persistence and not listening to Reese's wishes created a perceived threat of violence. Chris's attempts to change Reese's mind was manipulation. Chris's never-ending efforts became a form of coercion that intimidated Reese into saying "Yes." If Chris respected Reese, Chris would have stopped acting this way the first time Reese said "No." The threat of Chris acting out physically against Reese scared Reese into saying, "Yes."

Repeated attempts at sexual intimacy are common in relationships. When most people hear "No," do they completely give up on getting the person to engage in the sexual activity? No. People try to convince the partner why they "should" engage in the sexual activity with them. Excuses such as, "If you loved me," "If you cared about me," and "It will be fun" are a few of the many lines people use on a daily basis.

The other subtle form of manipulation is the diversionary tactic. When a person hears "No," they go back to engaging in a less threatening act of intimacy until trying again later on (similar to Chris in the previous story). For example, Chris wants to have sex, but Reese says no. What does Chris do? Chris gives Reese a backrub. As Reese is enjoying the backrub, Chris's hands begin to move down into Reese's pants. After a certain period of time, Chris brings up having sex with Reese again. Reese again says, "No." Chris returns to giving a backrub and the cycle continues.

Are you capable of being manipulative during intimacy? If so, make an effort to catch yourself before you disrespect another person's wishes. If someone wants sexual intimacy, the person will say, "Yes" the first time you ask. Trying to manipulate a partner into changing their decision about intimacy is a form of coercion.

Various forms of coercion are used against survivors. Child molesters prey on young children's minds and bodies to convince a child that the perpetrator's sexual acts are normal and healthy.

People with cognitive or communication disabilities are often sexually assaulted by trusted authority figures, including family members and professionals who are caretakers. We have also seen too many teachers, coaches, and religious figures take advantage of their positions of power to exploit children and adolescents. There are now laws that protect adults from exploitation by certain professionals based on their relationship and position of power over individuals who might be very vulnerable, e.g., correctional officers and inmates, doctors and patients, therapists and clients.

Across the country, laws exist to *protect adolescents* from sexual assault and exploitation by older individuals. However, teenagers often question the laws defining age and sexual activity. Many teenagers feel these laws take away their right to make choices. In reality, these laws gives adolescents more rights by helping protect young people from those who are more than willing to exploit them for their own gain.

Why does a minor need protection? The twenty-year-old trying to be sexually involved with a fourteen-year-old can have an advantage over the younger person. Through the experience of age, the older person can know how to manipulate a younger person. Manipulating the mind of a minor for sexual gain is a crime. Here is an example of coercion.

Tanner and Jace are dating. Jace knows Tanner has very low self-esteem. Jace knows Tanner bases Tanner's self-worth on their relationship. Jace believes if Jace stops dating Tanner, Tanner will become depressed and feel no self-worth.

As Jace tries to be intimate with Tanner, Tanner is not

ready. Tanner tells Jace, "No." Jace says, "You want to date me? Then you're going to do this with me. Otherwise, I am not going out with you. If I dump you, no one is going to get near you. Not after what I tell them. You will be worthless. I am the one person who understands you and who will treat you right. All you have to do is do this with me and everything will be okay."

Jace is knowingly manipulating Tanner by playing on Tanner's greatest fears. Jace is emotionally tearing Tanner down. Once Tanner is emotionally weakened, Jace uses intimacy as the tool to build a false sense of self-worth for Tanner.

Unfortunately, this scenario happens too frequently. If you know someone who will do anything with their partner just to stop the partner from breaking up with them, talk to the person. Help the person realize how valuable they are without needing that dating partner. Help the person learn that people who care about you will never treat you so horribly. Call a crisis line to get advice on how to help this person get out of a manipulative relationship.

 How about this?

Write down every "line" or excuse you can create that a person would use to manipulate a date into becoming sexually intimate. Then explain how the logic is flawed for each "line" or excuse.

Example No. 1

A partner says to a date, "Don't you think I'm attractive? If you found me attractive, you would want to do this with me."

Example No. 2

A person says to a longtime partner, "We have been dating over six months. This is only natural. If you loved me, you would do this."

Family and Friends

Sexual assault has a ripple effect among the people close to the survivor. Many may struggle with a wide range of emotions from guilt for not protecting their loved one to wanting to get revenge on the assailant. Family and friends should seek out support to help address these emotions and the pain they are feeling.

I was in college when sexual assault changed my life and my family forever. A note was taped to my door. The note said:

"Call Home IMMEDIATELY!" When I called, my mom answered and she said, "Mike, I have some bad news. Cheri has been raped." My sister, Cheri, had been raped! This could not be happening. I just started crying.

I wanted to kill the person who did this to my sister. Yes, I mean kill. I am telling you because you deserve to know the anger and rage sexual assault causes. More importantly, know it is normal to feel this way after a loved one has been assaulted. Did I act on my feelings? No! No one should. If I sought out revenge, I would have committed a crime and landed in jail. I would have made matters worse for everyone, especially for Cheri.

Within one year of my sister's assault, I went from being an honors student in college to almost being expelled for bad grades. I went from knowing exactly what I wanted in life to completely questioning everything. I searched for security and stability and found myself unstable and insecure.

How does this confusion happen? You never imagine this

horrific crime happening to a loved one, but suddenly, it does. You are shocked. You become overwhelmed with questions of, "How could this happen?" The fact that my sister's assailant was going to prison for a long time did not matter to me. I still had anger and rage building up inside. I felt guilty for not protecting my loved one.

All of my feelings and confusion were normal for the family member or friend of a sexual assault survivor. I felt like I had no place to turn for help. If you are affected by another person's assault, get counseling. Parents, siblings, and affected friends of an assault survivor often need professional help to teach them how to cope with this trauma.

How did the sexual assault of my sister change my perception of a rapist and the issue of sexual assault? When her assailant was being charged, I began learning about sexual assault laws. The law stated sexual assault is sexual contact without consent. Without consent? Even back then, I knew the only way you could definitely have consent was to ask.

I had never asked a woman before I kissed her. All of a sudden, I was looking at myself and saying, "Who am I to want to kill this rapist?" If I did anything with one of my dates and she didn't want it, I was similar to a rapist. I might have put a woman into an unwanted and nonconsensual situation.

Suddenly, the issue of sexual assault was not just about my sister being assaulted. My past was making me question my values and belief system. I wanted to make a change to ensure I never acted with disrespect toward a woman. After hearing Joseph Weinberg, a sexual assault activist, give a presentation on my college campus, I realized I could make a difference. I could make a difference in my life and the lives of others.

I began researching sexual assault. One of the first lessons I learned is that a sexual assault is a sexual assault. What do I mean? Whether someone you were hooking up with at a party forced their hand down your pants, a partner forced sexual intercourse against your will, or a stranger sexually assaulted you in a parking lot, the trauma can be horrific and the crime is a sexual assault.

I do not share the specifics of my sister's rape with audiences. No person needs to hear the details of a sexual assault. The mere thought of the rape should be disgusting enough without hearing the details of the actual horror.

How about this?

How can you help family and friends learn more about sexual assault and take the actions necessary to make a positive impact? Talk to your family and friends about dating, relationships, healthy intimacy, and sexual assault. The more people are aware, the more they have the opportunity to protect and help each other. Ask questions that will provoke conversation.

Example

Have you ever been uncomfortable on a date or when alone with someone in an intimate moment? Did you ever feel like someone took advantage of you in such a moment? Have you ever felt like you shouldn't have tried what you did with a partner?

While having this conversation, do not overly pry into a person's privacy. If a person has been assaulted, they may not want to talk about the assault in front of other people.

Every Survivor and Their Story Is Unique

The biggest mistake we can make in treating sexual assault survivors is looking down on them with pity. Survivors seek understanding and support. Show respect for the courage and strength the person has when sharing their experiences and honor their healing process.

Too often, society puts survivors into preset roles, ranging from quiet and scarred to outspoken and rebellious. The actual spectrum of survivors' experiences and healing cannot be accurately described by this limited range of behaviors.

The day I received the call about my sister being raped, I talked with her on the telephone. The first words from Cheri's mouth were, "How are you doing, Mike? Are you okay?" Am I okay? How could she be worried about me? A predator had raped her just hours earlier and she was worried about me? Do you see where I get my inspiration from? Open your eyes and your heart to survivors. You will have the chance to be inspired.

Society's Hidden Problem

There are millions of sexual assault survivors in our society. Those millions of survivors have families and friends. The result is a culture full of hurting people from a crime that no one wants to discuss. You can help change our culture. You can help people see the importance of this issue. You can help reduce the number of sexual assaults happening in the world. How? Get involved. Open up conversations with your family and friends. Challenge everyone to evaluate their beliefs about relationships and sexual assault.

CHAPTER 6: DO YOU UNDERSTAND?

Remember this:

- Coercion is a form of sexual assault.
- Sexual assault impacts survivors and their friends and family.
- Counseling can help survivors process their experiences and aid in their healing.
- Know that anyone can be a "rapist."
- Give survivors respect!

Try this:

Next time you are with a friend or a group of friends, ask them all what they think is the best way to date or to begin a sexually intimate relationship. Ask them to describe what they think about sexual assault. Could it happen to them? Could anyone they know commit this crime? Open their minds and their hearts to create change.

Bonus

 Strictly Students: Could someone pressure or coerce you? Find out at www.canikissyou.com/students.

 Parents' Pointers: Tell your teenagers, "The wait is worth it." As a parent, are you waiting? Go to www.canikissyou.com/parents.

 Teachers' Tool: What about the survivor in your classroom? Go to www.canikissyou.com/educators.

my**NOTES**:

7

Are You Aware?
Will You Intervene?
Mind, Body, and Bystander Intervention

To help reduce the likelihood of someone you know being affected by sexual assault, develop an acute awareness for the issues concerning sexual assault.

Sexual Assault Awareness

The root word "aware" defines the concept of awareness. By being more aware, each of us can help ourselves and those around us to see potentially dangerous situations. Awareness helps us keep our eyes and ears open for trouble—without assuming that we can always "prevent" an attack. The more aware each of us is, the less likely an attack can occur.

What about "prevention"? The word "prevention" is widely misused in educating people about sexual assault. The root word "prevent" implies you can prevent all sexual assaults from happening to you. You can't! There is no 100 percent effective way to "prevent" a sexual assault.

By using the word "prevention," people might assume the survivor "could have prevented the assault if . . . ," thus placing blame on the survivor for not being able to stop the assault from occurring. We never want to blame the survivor. The survivor is never at fault. For this reason, awareness is the correct word to use when discussing trying to raise society's understanding of sexual assault.

Gender and Sexual Orientation Stereotypes

Many stereotypes of sexual assault create dangerous societal beliefs. One of the biggest myths is that "sexual assault is a man forcing himself on a woman." The use of the word "woman" implies that sexual assault only happens to women. The use of the word "man" implies that men are always the perpetrators. While the majority of assaults do fall into this category, assaults occur every day that do not fit this profile. Survivors and perpetrators include people of all genders, sexual orientations, ethnicities, and socioeconomic backgrounds.

Did you know that same-gender sexual assaults (man-on-man and woman-on-woman) have been perpetrated by heterosexual individuals? Sexual attraction is not the motivation behind sexual assault. The crime of sexual assault is a crime of power and degradation, of one person forcing their wants onto another person—for personal gratification and/or to humiliate and degrade another person.

Hate crimes against non-heterosexuals have involved heterosexuals sexually assaulting a gay, lesbian, bisexual, or pansexual individual. These tragic crimes are another example of how sex and sexuality are used as devastating weapons in a crime of sexual assault.

One of the reasons survivors are afraid to speak out is because of the standards society has created for gender. Blanket gender statements create tremendous suffering. Some people in our society try to place blame on the survivor for not acting like their gender stereotype.

"A real lady would never allow herself to be in that situation."

Are all women supposed to live according to one person's standard? No. Unfortunately, our society has been known to imply that women should live their lives a specific way. Think of the wording used in the comment about "a real lady." Do some women fit the profile of being "a fake lady"? Of course not. Each woman is her own being. What harm is done by using the words "would never allow"? If you are a survivor and you hear this statement, you could ask yourself if you "allowed" the assault to happen. Asking such a question can begin to build guilt inside you for the actions of your assailant. No survivor deserves this extra burden of guilt to overcome.

"The guy is gay if he let another person rape him."

As we mentioned previously, people of all sexual orientations have been assaulted. Saying anyone "let" an assault happen is an oxymoron. Sexual assault is a crime against your will. Millions of men of all sexual orientations have been sexually assaulted. The assailants have been men and women.

Our society knows men have been assaulted. By making such careless and cruel comments as expressed above, we are creating a repressive environment for survivors.

A survivor is a survivor—regardless of gender, race, ethnicity, appearance, or sexual orientation.

Your RIGHTS

On a date or when alone with someone in a sexually intimate moment, you and your partner both have the following rights:

- To have your voice respected.
- To have your boundaries respected.
- To be free of coercion of any kind (including no guilt or pity being placed on you).

- To have an equal say in all choices (where the two of you are going, etc.).
- To feel safe and comfortable.
- To end the date or intimate moment at any second you choose.

Alan Berkowitz, consultant and author, shared with me that it is important to consider the following guidelines:

- Avoid spending time with anyone who wants to control what you do and how you spend your time.
- Be aware of your surroundings and have a plan for getting help or leaving if a situation becomes dangerous.
- Don't be afraid to assert yourself physically and verbally, even at the risk of upsetting the other person. Research shows that individuals who resist are less likely to suffer harm when assaulted.

If you think your partner is not honoring your rights, end the date and/or relationship. Have someone pick you up. By ending the date and being picked up by someone you trust, you are able to help yourself quickly get into a safer and more supportive environment—which you deserve.

Having to drive back home with a person you are uncomfortable with and/or fear can lead to an unsafe situation.

How about this?

Have a group of people watch at least two reality shows this evening where intimacy is commonly discussed and/ or occurs. During the shows, no one can talk to each other. Instead, write down each sign of disrespect you notice a person on the show exhibiting while discussing intimacy, a relationship, and/or during an actual scene of sexual intimacy. Include all forms of disrespect (both for their own being and toward their partners).

When the shows are done, share your observations with the other individuals who watched the shows with you. Count how many times all of you picked up the same signs of disrespect. Decide what the people on the television show could have done to show respect toward each other while still having fun on the date.

The most effective defense against sexual assault is awareness. By watching for signs of trouble, you are better equipped to react before the trouble begins. If you use every form of awareness and self-defense available, will you be completely safe from being sexually assaulted? No. Will you be able to stop every sexual assault from ever happening to another person? No.

Bystander or Caring Person?

If you could stop a sexual assault from taking place, would you? Most people say, "I would never let someone else be sexually assaulted." Yet the same person is likely to watch a person at a party take a highly intoxicated individual into a back room. The same observer may stand idly by as a group of friends brag about how to "keep the beers coming to Devon. If Devon keeps drinking, one of us is going to get some tonight."

When you hear a person talk with disrespect toward a partner or a person at a party, what do you do? If you saw a person trying to take advantage of another person, what would you do? What if the person was not your friend? Friend or not, do not be a bystander. Are you afraid of embarrassing yourself by speaking out? If someone treats another person with disrespect, do not concern yourself with the disrespectful person's image of you. Concern yourself with the danger another person is being placed in.

> Imagine leaving a party and saying to your friend, "I'm worried about Phoenix. Phoenix has been drinking a lot, and who knows what could happen." The next morning, you learn that Phoenix was sexually assaulted at the party. How would you feel? The assault is not your fault. The assailant is at fault. Yet maybe you could have helped stop the assault from happening to Phoenix.

Sadly, this scenario happens every weekend, and most often, we won't realize it. Normally, you are not going to know that Phoenix was sexually assaulted because Phoenix is not likely to tell you.

> You are at a party with friends. You see someone trying to take Carson, a really intoxicated person, home and talking about how "I am getting some tonight." What do you do?

Go up to the person and say, "Thanks for offering to take Carson home. It was very nice of you to offer, but I will take care of getting Carson home." By intervening, you helped protect your friend from possibly being sexually assaulted. Friend or not, you can help protect a person from being sexually assaulted.

Will You Tell?

> You are in college and live in a residence hall. Everyone knows each other on the floor. The residence hall has a 12:00 a.m. curfew for having guests leave the residence halls. As you walk down the hall at 1:00 a.m., you hear a voice you don't recognize coming from a friend's room. You know it is not the voice of your friend. Do you tell the R.A. (Residence Advisor)?

Can this unknown person present a danger to the others living or staying on that floor and/or in the residence hall? Yes. What if, on their way out of the building, the person sexually assaults a student? These types of sexual assaults have occurred on college campuses across the country. Inform an R.A. about the person inside the room. If you are afraid of someone learning you "told" the R.A., then ask the R.A. not to tell anyone that you were the person who reported the violation. By helping reduce the risk of a sexual assault, you are helping keep everyone in the residence hall safer. Curfews and "locked door" policies were created to protect students living on campus and in residence halls.

What is a "locked door" policy or law? On college campuses, entrance doors to the residence halls are locked to keep strangers and dangerous individuals out. Frequently, students prop the doors open to let someone inside the dorm without having to enter through the main entrance, for example, to sneak a partner into their room.

Unfortunately, sexual assaults happen each year when assailants sneak in through these propped-open doors. You can help protect yourself and your fellow students by respecting these important safety policies on campus.

So You Just Watched?

What if you did nothing as you watched a sexual assault or a gang rape occur? By doing nothing to stop or report an assault, you are helping enable the assailants in their crime. What if you were the victim or a close friend of the victim? Would you want someone to call for help? By calling the authorities, you can do the right thing and help protect another human being.

Unfortunately, too many people look away or keep watching as a sexual assault is being set up or is occurring because they are waiting for someone else to do something.

What if a person isn't stepping in because they are afraid of confrontation? Most people are not afraid of confrontation when they believe the confrontation is worth getting involved over. Will children argue with their parents over an issue they know they will not win? Yes. Why? Because the child believes in the principle of what they are arguing about with their parents. In the case of a person in danger right in front of you at a party or event, is the person's safety and life worth you taking on some form of confrontation for them? Yes. We are about to arm you with specific steps to take for helping to reduce the level of confrontation involved.

In moments like this at parties or other venues, have you ever heard someone say, "That is none of my business"? You know better than to do nothing. You know that every person deserves dignity and respect. You know that *every person is worth your effort to step in and intervene*. Consequently, what is happening in front of you is your business, especially when someone is trying to harm another person whom you could help.

Four Steps to Bystander Intervention

Why is stepping in to help called "Bystander Intervention"? Because you are no longer choosing to watch as a bystander, and instead, you are making the choice to do something: intervene. You are a bystander intervening to help another person. Awesome!

Here are Four Steps to Bystander Intervention:

1. Dignity and Respect
2. Team Up and Check In
3. Distract
4. Stay Calm

EXAMPLE:

You are at a party. Landry is trying to get Marley, who appears to be severely incapacitated due to either the influence of alcohol and/or drugs, alone in a back room at the party. You do not know Landry nor Marley. You do know that typically people go into the backrooms to "hook up" and/or engage in sexual intimacy. Following is how you can apply the four steps of bystander intervention in this situation.

1. Dignity and Respect

Since you know every person deserves to be treated with dignity and respect, you know Marley deserves dignity and respect, including right now. Since Marley does not appear to be of sound mind, you recognize Marley is not able to consent to any sexual activity with Landry.

You see and understand the danger.

2. Team Up and Check In

As is typical, you are out with friends. Go to three or four friends and ask, *"Hey, there is a situation over there that is really concerning me. I want to check in and make sure everything is okay with someone who seems very intoxicated. Will you come with me and back me up?"*

Having your friends with you when you check in with Landry and Marley often increases your confidence and comfort level. Tell your friends you want them to help you intervene with Landry and check in with Marley. You will approach the two of them like you would anyone else whom you really want to talk with.

3. Distract

At least one of you will start talking with Landry, asking Landry where Landry is from and whom Landry came with. See whether you can separate Landry completely from Marley. Talking points that can often engage people at a party include: music, sports, movies, school/work, and even the weather.

At the same time that some of you begin engaging with Landry, at least one of you will start talking with Marley. Ask Marley whether everything is okay and where Marley's friends are. Knowing where Marley's friends are enables you to connect Marley back up with friends. You can let the friends know what you were observing and your concerns. Now the friends can help too.

If you are at a bar or club, you could also let security and/or bouncers know you are concerned about what you are watching and ask them to check in on Landry. Focus them on the person who appears to be setting up a dangerous and potentially criminal situation.

4. Stay Calm

If Landry starts to get upset and/or begins to threaten you over checking in on Marley, stick together with your friends as a team and stay calm. Deescalate the situation as much as possible by letting Landry know that you just want to make sure Marley is okay.

The above example is only one possibility of how you can step in and intervene. Get your friends together and discuss the ways you could help each other intervene with different situations. List all the possible strategies you could utilize for creating distractions. The more tools you have as options, the more effective you will become at intervening.

Consider the possibilities of how many lives you and your friends could positively impact!

How about this?

Watch the movie *The Accused* and discuss who could have intervened. Why do you think this crime happened the way it did? Why didn't more people do something?

Can you think of cases in the news where people have failed to intervene? Examples of cases you can research online include the sexual assault case involving students from Steubenville High School in Steubenville, Ohio and the sexual assault case involving students from Richmond High School in Richmond, California.

Tools of Self-Defense!

Please notice the keyword of "self-defense." This section of the book is not a guideline for how "not to be sexually assaulted." As we've discussed previously, the only person who can guarantee a sexual assault does not happen is the assailant—by never attempting a sexual assault.

The following section is for those individuals who want more information about self-defense options and strategies.

Body and Clothes

Your body and your clothes are helpful forms of defense against an attack. A belt, a shoe, a key, your finger, and many other items on your being can seriously hurt an attacker. A course on self-defense is the best avenue for learning these skills.

Self-Defense Devices

Self-defense mechanisms such as mace, whistles, blow horns, and special alarms can be great options to possess for moments when danger is imminent or occurring. Call your local police department to ensure that the device you are carrying or are considering buying is legal. The handling of devices is essential to their effectiveness. Self-defense devices have been used against survivors. Carefully read over the instructions to use and handle the device correctly and safely.

If you carry a self-defense device, or if you are trained in how to fight back, do not fall into the trap of thinking you are always 100 percent safe. Attackers look for people who are not aware of their surroundings and situation. A person who is not paying attention is seen as being more vulnerable in the eyes of an assailant. Try to look for signs of trouble before they occur. Be alert. Constantly use your skills of awareness.

"Safety" Space

If someone tries to make a move on you without asking, immediately create a physical space between the two of you. This is called your "safety" space. Separate yourself from the person. If you are sitting together on a date, move farther away from the person. The physical space between the two of you provides a safer environment for you. The "safety" space helps create a "stop sign" effect.

As you quickly create a physical space, speak with a strong voice to let the person know you do not want the intimate action they are trying. You can almost always begin turning someone down by saying, "Stop. I really appreciate that you are interested in me, but. . . ."

Explain how you do not get intimately involved with anyone until you are ready. Share how you expect your partner to talk with you about what they want to do before trying it with you. Most people have never received an education on healthy dating. Provide an opportunity to role model healthy and respectful behaviors.

If the person tries to make a move on you in a disrespectful manner (trying to force you into a position or quickly moving upon you, etc.), scream "Stop! Get away from me!" as loudly as you can.

While screaming, try to create your "safety" space. Do not worry about embarrassing the other person by your screaming. The person was not respecting you. Protect yourself!

Plan Ahead

Planning ahead can greatly prepare you for threatening situations. Think of how you would try to defend yourself in various situations.

Decide your boundaries for intimacy before you begin dating or start a relationship. Having set boundaries helps diminish the level of confusion you might feel when you experience feelings of attraction toward another person. By having set boundaries, you are less likely to be asking yourself, "Should I do this with my date?" By having your boundaries decided, you will know the answer to the question before the situation occurs. Training your mind is as important as training your body.

 How about this?

Write down your dating and intimacy boundaries. Write why you believe in setting the standards you have chosen. Before you go on each date, read this list out loud to yourself. By hearing your own boundaries and the reasoning, you will place the boundaries at the forefront of your mind.

Example

I do not kiss someone on a first date for two reasons. First, I do not want to give my date the impression that dating me means guaranteed intimacy. Second, after only one date, I don't know you well enough to begin intimacy. If you like me for who I am, you will wait until I am completely comfortable with you.

Shock

By learning self-defense moves, utilizing proper devices, and being completely aware of your surroundings, you help increase the chance of protecting yourself. Since 100 percent prevention does not exist, you *can* still be sexually assaulted. When an assault happens, you do not know exactly what you will do or will be capable of. You could try to scream and have no sound come out of your mouth. The trauma of being assaulted can cause shock and disable your body's defense mechanisms (your muscles freeze, you lose your voice).

When a person asks a survivor, "Why didn't you say, 'No'?" or "Why didn't you kick the assailant?" the person is assuming that reacting to an assault is a natural process. The notion that humans under stress have a natural "fight or flight" reaction is incorrect. The reality is humans instinctually have a "freeze, fight, or flight" reaction. During a traumatic experience, the body and the mind can shut down (the natural instinct to "freeze"). Shock and trauma can severely limit a victim's ability to process what is happening and respond accordingly. Shock can limit your ability to react physically to your assailant. You cannot blame the survivor or hold the survivor accountable for their immediate reaction during this awful crime.

Responsible Change

One of the greatest opportunities for each of us to reduce sexual assault is by helping our society transform our culture into one that is based on respect and consent.

You have the ability to inspire change in people by helping individuals see the need for respect. Listen for peers, family, and friends who use language that degrades others based on sexual orientation, gender, and/or sexual choices a person has made. When you hear a person victim blaming, help the person understand that survivors deserve to be admired. Once you open a person's mind or heart to wanting to learn more, give them a great book to read on the issue of sexual assault, relationships, and dating. (See the suggested reading list at the end of this book.)

Utilize all of the resources available. Be sure that your efforts to change people's views are producing positive results. Repetition is one of the most effective education tools. Periodically discuss healthy dating, relationships, consent, and sexual assault with family and friends.

CHAPTER 7: ARE YOU AWARE? WILL YOU INTERVENE?

Remember this:

- 100 percent prevention does *not* exist.
- There is no singular profile of a survivor.
- Intervene. Each person is worthy.
- Awareness, body, and clothes can be used for self-defense.
- Be responsible in educating others.

Try this:

Do searches on the Internet under "sexual assault awareness." Visit at least twenty different Internet sites and write down ten ideas, facts, or concepts you did not know. Education is a lifelong process.

Bonus

 Strictly Students: Find the #1 self-defense move at www.canikissyou.com/students.

 Parents' Pointers: Have *fun* creating your child's safety space at www.canikissyou.com/parents.

 Teachers' Tool: Get the "What is in here?" exercise at www.canikissyou.com/educators.

my**NOTES**:

Your Next Date
What Are You Focused On?

As we discussed in the Introduction to this book, a **date** is defined as partners with an intimate attraction (and/or considering an intimate attraction) spending time together. A date can include a first date, a couple hanging out (single or committed), a "hook-up," and/or a group of couples spending time together.

Dating should be respectful, fun, exciting, and exploratory in nature. This chapter is dedicated to helping each person enjoy the dating process and to creating the best scenarios for getting to spend time together with someone you are interested in as a partner.

On a date, how can you help create an ideal setting where both of you feel respected, are comfortable, and are having fun learning about each other?

First, keep that one special word at the forefront of your mind: respect. Make sure you always act with respect toward yourself and your partner. Watch for any signs of disrespect from either of you.

Watch for all types of power plays. Are you making decisions together, or is one person trying to decide everything? Below are a few choices you can make when planning a date.

Groups

Going out with a group of friends for a first date can be good and bad. If the group is laid back and not interested in any specific outcomes regarding your relationship with your date, the group setting could be very positive. The two of you are less likely to have any expectations of intimacy in a group setting.

If the group you go out with is capable of encouraging the two of you to "hook up" or "get together," this group behavior would be a very disrespectful environment for the two of you. With peer pressure being applied, many people are likely to be persuaded into lowering their standards. You might try harder for a "connection between the two of you" just to please the group.

 How about this?

What are comments that friends and peers can make to pressure a couple into sexual intimacy? What will you say if someone makes these comments to you? Role play with a group of friends.

Have everyone try to pressure you about being intimate with your date. Before responding, notice how this pressure makes you feel. What do you want to say? Then, decide what is the best and most respectful response to the pressure being put on you by your friends.

Example

Skylar is about to go on a date with Jess. Before the date, Skylar is talking with a friend, Dallas. Dallas says to Skylar, "Jess wants you. You need to 'get some' tonight."

What does Skylar want to say? Does Skylar want to say,

"Oh, yeah"?

What should Skylar say to Dallas? What if Skylar says, "Dallas, I like Jess a lot, but I am not going to assume Jess wants me. If I think you are right, I'll ask Jess before we do anything. I am not out only to 'get some' from Jess. I assume you don't want me to treat dates that way, do you, Dallas?"

Establish the Rule of Talking

How do you create an atmosphere of equal respect when you go on a date? Talk openly and honestly. Talking will help you learn whether the other person respects you. Plus, talking helps you learn about the other person (likes, dislikes, quirks, etc.).

Create an atmosphere of conversation before you go on the date. If you are asking the other person out, let the person know you want them involved in the entire process of planning the date so you can ensure that the two of you have an awesome time. As you talk and decide what you are going to do together, you will be building a foundation for open conversation throughout the date.

Listening

Are you listening to your partner and what the person is sharing? How does this person talk about life, you, family, friends, activities, and/or passions? Is what the person is saying matching the type of person you really enjoy spending time with?

A fun question employers will sometimes ask themselves before hiring a teammate is, "If I were stuck in an airport with this person for twenty-four hours, would I thoroughly enjoy myself or be dreading how much more time was left before I could get away from this person?"

Another helpful question to ask is, "How do I feel about myself when I am around this person?" As we discussed in Chapter 3, you are a "10." Do you feel like less than a "10" when you are with this person? If so, know you deserve to be with a person who does not make you feel less than you are.

A date is an audition. You could be two wonderful people who simply are not the right fit for a wonderful relationship. You don't want to feel the pressure of "I've got to make this work." If the two of you are not the right fit, do not take it personally. Be respectful in letting your partner know the two of you don't feel like a great fit. Be sure to thank the person for the opportunity to get to know them.

Time of the Day
Go on a date in the early afternoon and enjoy the many public places that are perfect for exploring during the daytime. When other people can see you, such as in a public place, both people are less likely to "try" making a move on the other person in a disrespectful manner. Additionally, there is much more to do during the day (parks, miniature golf, athletic events, etc.).

Be Creative
Stay away from the typical "movie" date. Do you want to learn about your date? While watching a movie, how can you get to know each other? Watching a movie eliminates all opportunities to talk and learn what the other person is like.

Think of a fun and simple activity where you can talk together throughout the event. If you are interested in each other, you can pick the silliest activity and you will have a blast together. Even if you are both horrible at bowling, imagine how much fun you would have laughing together and talking as you bowled. Write down all of the creative activities you could do on a creative date.

Meet Your Date
Meet the person at the exact location of the date so each of you

are in control of arriving and leaving. If you are in an uncomfortable situation, you are in control of leaving.

If you are at a date's house, your date has more control. When someone is in their own home, they are much more likely to feel comfortable taking risks. Risk is not a good factor for a date. Avoid setting up the date to occur at a house.

How about this?

What can you do on a date that costs little or no money and does not involve intimacy? Think of creative dating ideas that are healthy, fun, and inexpensive. Remove the financial stress of dating.

Example
Go on a picnic to the beach.

Stay Close to Home
If your date is taking place at a location not easy for you to get home from, what will you do if the date starts to go bad? What will you do if you don't feel comfortable or enjoy being around your date? Avoid traveling long distances. Stay close to home.

Who Pays?
For some people, who pays for the date can imply who is in control. When one person pays, some people feel they "owe" the partner a kiss (or more) for paying. You do not owe your date a kiss or any form of intimacy. Are you an object for sale? No. You are a priceless person.

When two people are equal, they only owe each other respect. Date a person you consider to be your equal. Treat all of your dates like equals and expect your date to treat you as an equal. To avoid this perception of control completely, split the costs! Sharing the expenses of the date eliminates this entire concern for "owing" sexual intimacy.

If you are the person who requested the date, most dates will expect you to pay. If you are paying for everything, then do not expect anything in return.

Before going on the date, discuss how to pay for the activities. Some people are concerned that if they offer to pay for a date, they will offend the dating partner. In a respectful manner, explain your reasoning for wanting to pay. Here is an example of a person offering to pay for half of the date:

> "When I go on a date, I believe in treating you with total respect. Making you pay for everything is not respectful, and it would be selfish on my part. Plus, it is not fair to you, especially when I am having a great time being with you. Therefore, I would like to pay for my half of the date. I hope my paying my half is okay with you, because I am really looking forward to this date."

If your date is offended by this explanation, take this as a warning sign. You clearly showed the person respect, and you nicely explained your reasoning. You even told your date you are excited about going on the date. If the person becomes stuck on doing things their way, you may have a reason to be concerned. This person may be selfish or self-centered. Talk with your date to learn why they do not agree with you or why they are not willing to compromise with you.

Even if your date turns down your offer to pay, the person can tell you care about them and respect them. You have set a very positive and unique tone for the date.

No Pity Dates

One of the most uncaring actions you can take is to go on a Pity Date or to give someone a Pity Kiss.

A Pity Date is when you are not interested in the other person. You go on the date only because you do not want to hurt the person's feelings. A Pity Date is extremely disrespectful to the other person's feelings. You are setting your date up for failure. Have the courage to do the right thing. Tell the person you are not interested, and express how you appreciate their asking you out.

Giving your date a Pity Kiss is a disrespectful and dishonest act. If your date asks you for a kiss and you do not want to kiss the person, do not kiss the person! When you say, "Yes," your date thinks you wanted the kiss. By saying, "Yes," you are misleading your partner. Always be honest.

Saying "No" to Being Asked

If a person asks you for a kiss and you don't want to kiss, appreciate the respect being given to you by the person asking. Tell the person, "Thank you for asking. I am honored, but . . . " and then fill in the reason. Explain the reason in a caring fashion. If you are not attracted to the person, say, "I don't feel a connection between the two of us."

STOP the Kiss

You ask your date for a kiss or any intimate act. The person says, "Yes" in a hesitant fashion (not sounding as though they want to). What do you do? Tell your date, "If you are not comfortable, that is okay. The last thing I want is to make you feel uncomfortable. We don't have to." As pathetic as a Pity Kiss is, you don't want to be the recipient of one.

Hold on to Your Standards

Hold on to your standards at all times. If a date tries to convince you to do something you don't want to do, be strong in your statements. You are a "10," so demand the respect of a "10." Once you have set high standards for yourself, you never want to question or lower your standards.

CHAPTER 8: YOUR NEXT DATE

Remember this:

- Show *respect* for yourself and your partner.
- Be aware of potential power plays.
- Start talking *before* the date.
- Be honest at all times.
- Honor your standards.

Try this:
Come up with more examples of how one person could try to control his or her date. Next, decide how to avoid or handle those situations.

Bonus

 Strictly Students: Discover three fun, low-cost dating ideas at www.canikissyou.com/students.

 Parents' Pointers: Find two powerful statements at www.canikissyou.com/parents to share with your teenager as he or she leaves for a date.

 Teachers' Tool: Get the "No Way" Activity at www.canikissyou.com/educators.

my**NOTES**:

9

What Influences You?
Stop & Notice

Before and during a date, what are you filling your mind with? Are you listening to all your friends who are giving you advice? Friends can share well-intentioned, but very misguided, suggestions such as:

- How to impress your date.
- How to play the dating game.

Impressing Your Date

Do not try to impress your dating partner. Trying to impress other people leads to misleading behavior from you. Be the same person on a date that you are when you are hanging out with friends. If someone is going to like you, you want the person to like *you*.

A common example of trying to impress a partner is after finding out your partner's interests, you state how you have the same interests—even when you do not. For example, your partner loves horror movies. You tell your partner you also love horror movies. In reality, you hate horror movies. You only said it to try to connect with your partner.

By acting differently, you are not being your authentic self. You are lowering yourself to playing a game. Respect yourself. Be proud of who you are as a person.

Playing the Dating Game

In a game, you have two competitors going against each other. Both competitors are trying to win at the other competitor's cost. A great competitor does everything to play directly against the opponent's weaknesses. Turning a date into a game is a bad decision.

You can turn a date into a game without even realizing it. Do you or your friends use any of the following phrases?

- "Did you hit on them?"
- "Did you score?"
- "Play your cards right and you'll get some."

These expressions are commonly used in our society. Each phrase shows disregard for another human being. The words can sometimes be seen as violent or at least careless ("hit," "score," "get some"). Your friends might say, "They are only words," but words are powerful and lasting.

Your mind remembers the last message you send it. When your mind hears the above messages, it subconsciously focuses on scoring and winning. One person focusing on winning and scoring creates a dangerous dating atmosphere for the person who is going to lose. Eliminate all comparisons to a game and create a *fun* date for both of you.

 How about this?

Write down every comparison between dating and a game. Write down how people use these comparisons in everyday conversation. What references in the entertainment industry promote "The Game"? What songs? What specific lyrics? Which characters on shows and in films? Can you think of entire movies that promote this poor treatment of partners? Challenge the logic and common sense behind each comparison and reference to "The Game." Explain the dangers and contradictions in using each analogy. Discuss how the mentality of "The Game" goes completely against having mutually wanted and agreed upon sexual intimacy (consent).

Example

"Did you score?" On the date, is there a scoreboard behind you? Each time you get what you want, does the scoreboard change in your favor? What if you disrespect your partner? Does your score get lowered for violating the rules? Can you get banned for life?

Peer Pressure

Do you realize how much peer pressure can influence the minds of two people going on a date? Analyze the pre-date advice Alex and Blake get from their friends in the following example:

Alex is hoping Blake is really cool. Alex would love for the two of them to "get it on" later in the night. Blake is attracted to Alex and hopes Alex feels the same. Blake wants to get to know Alex better. Blake wants to know whether Alex is a great person.

Alex's friends are saying how to set up the date so Blake is melting in Alex's hands and is totally hot for Alex. Blake's friends are saying what to wear and how to use body language to draw Alex in. Alex's friends are saying to get

Blake a little drunk to help Blake "loosen up." Blake's friends are saying to make sure you don't appear to be too "easy." Alex's friends are saying how to take control. Blake is being told how to play the game of being coy by letting Alex think Alex has control.

Does the scenario between Alex and Blake sound complicated or too simple? Think about two people you know who fit these profiles. Think about the people you know who have been on this exact date. The scenario between Alex and Blake happens every night of the week.

Did you notice how none of the friends were concerned about the dating partner's wants or needs? Did you see how the friends pushed their own goals onto Alex and Blake? Peers will assume you have the same standards as they do (moral, ethical, sexual, etc.). Even though you know you are different from each of your friends, you start to forget your true self. You start to focus on everything your friends are saying. Suddenly, you have new goals and strategies for the date. Your motivation for the date has centered on the messages your friends have left in your mind.

You might be saying to yourself, "I would never do that!" When your friends are giving you advice, you do not notice the mental shift taking place in your mind. Alex and Blake are not purposely saying to themselves, "Forget what I was thinking before I talked with my friends. I am going to be self-centered like my friends are saying." The mental shift happens in your subconscious.

To ensure that you do not allow this shift to occur in your mind, watch and listen for peer pressure. Once you recognize negative influences, you have the ability to block these harmful thought patterns. Family members, co-workers, and teammates can all offer negative advice without even realizing it. Watch and listen for negative influences so you can make the choice to keep negatives out of your mind!

IMPORTANT TO READ BEFORE CONTINUING:

Since we are about to discuss alcohol, drugs, and other influences, we need to stress an important discussion we had back in Chapter 3.

The following insights and suggestions are to help create the healthiest, safest environment for a person in a dating situation and should never be used to place blame or responsibility on a survivor for an assailant's actions.

If you make a choice that goes against your better judgment or could be considered by some people to make you more vulnerable to someone doing harm to you, know the person who does the harm to you is the person responsible for the harm. Not you! Just because you made what might be perceived as a poor choice, it never gives another person the right to harm you in any way.

Alcohol and Drugs

What other influences can affect a date? Introducing alcohol or drugs into a dating situation can be extremely dangerous! Alcohol and drugs change the chemistry of your mind and body. Once the chemistry in your mind and body is changed, you do not have the ability to think or react as soundly as you did when you were sober.

You will have difficulty making respectful choices. You might find yourself behaving in ways you would not approve of if you were sober. You might struggle to know the difference between right and wrong. The effects of alcohol and drugs may make you more susceptible to taking harmful actions against another person.

When consuming alcohol and drugs, you may take risks that put other people in danger. You may take risks that put you in danger. Your cloudy mental and incapacitated physical state makes you much less likely to be aware of danger or trouble approaching you. All of these factors can lead to an unhealthy dating atmosphere.

> Imagine drinking on a date. Toward the end of the evening, you bring your date back to your place. As the two of you are kissing, you feel a false sense of "confidence." You decide to "surprise" your date by making a very fast move toward touching them in a private area. After you begin the touching, your dating partner yells, "Stop! What are you doing? How dare you touch me like that?" You just sexually assaulted your date.

If you had been sober, you might not have acted the way you did. However, you weren't sober and you assaulted your date. You can't reverse what you did. The fact that you were intoxicated does not excuse your behavior. Why? You took the actions.

You can only apologize. What could you have done? Made the safer choice and stayed sober. The vast majority of reported sexual assaults involve the use of alcohol and/or drugs!

 How about this?

> What are reasons that friends use for drinking or using drugs on a date or at a party? Write as many reasons as you can think of. How can you counter this way of thinking with reasonable logic?

Example

"I can't relax or have fun on a date without a few drinks in me." If you can't have fun with your date without drinking, why are you going on the date with that person?

Being Taken Advantage of

Every weekend, sexual assaults are reported where a person wakes up from being passed out and finds someone on top of them engaged in a sexual act, or they just wake up feeling extremely disoriented because they feel as though someone had sex with them. Are both of these scenarios frightening? Yes. The survivor does not have control over their body and may not even be conscious. Yet someone else chooses to take advantage of an incapacitated and vulnerable person by engaging in sexual activity when they are unconscious or semiconscious. This disregard for another human is indefensible.

Do you know the scariest part? Lots of people engage in similar behavior. Have you ever heard a person say, "Get your date a little drunk; it will help loosen them up"? This person is encouraging someone to take advantage of another person.

If you are intimate with a person who is extremely intoxicated or high to the point of not being of sound mind, you are acting without consent. A mumbled "Yes" response, or a nod of the head from an incapacitated person is not consent. If a drunk person says, "I want to have sex with you," it isn't consent. To give consent, the partner must be aware of what is being asked of them and they must be engaging in that act freely and voluntarily. When you know a person has been drinking or taking drugs to the point of not being of sound mind, do not become sexually involved with the person!

Someone "being exploited or taken advantage of" is almost

always a sexual assault. "Taking advantage" of a vulnerable person due to age, disability, or incapacitation due to drugs or alcohol is always wrong.

People will ask, "But what if the person really wants me when they are drunk?" If a person truly "wants you," then the person will still "want you" the next day when they are sober and of sound mind! Show respect and wait.

If your date wants you to get intoxicated or enter a state of not being of sound mind, ask yourself and your date, "Why?" A person who cares about you will not encourage you to lose control of your decision-making capabilities.

Drugs Used to Facilitate Sexual Assaults

The most dangerous drug is the one you do not know you have in your system. This can happen when you accept a drug from someone to get high without recognizing the drug or understanding the effects of the drug or when someone intentionally spikes your drink or food with a drug. When drinking alcohol, depending on the drink, it can be very difficult to detect anything wrong with your drink until it's too late. You have no idea you are being drugged. You could be drinking non-alcoholic beverages such as juice or soda and still be drugged. Bystanders will often think that you've just had too much to drink, not realizing that your behavior is actually inconsistent with the amount of alcohol consumed. Suspects in these cases will often act like the good Samaritan and offer to drive you home.

Devices have been created to detect these drugs. For example, coasters and dip sticks have been developed that will show whether certain drugs are in your beverage. Are these devices reliable? They might be. However, the real issue is that people are just not thinking logically or cautiously when drinking and having fun. There are better ways to watch out for each other.

When someone puts a drug into a person's drink, whether as a prank or to set that person up for a sexual assault or a robbery, it is a crime.

Parties and Entertainment Venues

At parties, entertainment venues, and concerts, more and more sexual assaults are being committed with the aid of drugs. In those environments, the rush from being around a bunch of people your age can give you a false sense of invincibility. When you are having tons of fun, you believe nothing can go wrong.

To have the most fun at these places, keep yourself alert and aware of your setting at all times. Do not put your beverage down or let someone else handle it. If you start to feel as if you're becoming intoxicated, take action! Get a trusted individual to take you home. Date rape drugs can kill! If you suspect you have ingested one, consider seeking medical attention and ask a trusted individual to keep an eye on you.

Imagine your beverage as a precious item that means everything to you—*precious* because it is going into your body. If a drug gets into your system, your life can be shattered. Be careful. Your life is precious!

Mob Mentality

Gang rapes can occur at parties. How can multiple people convince themselves to sexually assault the same person? Mob mentality. Individually, if each of the assailants were alone with the individual on a date, they may not have tried to sexually assault the person. However, when the assailants got into a group setting, they acted according to the group's behavior.

Two, three, four, five, or more friends are encouraging each person to "do it." Each person is being cheered on to engage in sexual activity with someone who is vulnerable because of their young age, drugs and alcohol or even forcibly. The group might say, "Have fun with them. They aren't even going to notice." The group keeps egging each person on. Gradually, several people start to believe in the group's behaviors and actions. The old "Everyone else is doing it; why not me?" philosophy starts to enter another person's mind. In the end, that person becomes an assailant. They sexually assault a person through the horrid act of a gang rape.

Arrogance

Why is arrogance being discussed in a section about drugs and alcohol? Arrogance can act like a "built-in drug." It makes you think everyone wants to do what you want to do. If you believe everyone wants what you want, you might try to take actions that affect another person without asking. If you have an arrogant friend, help the person see the need to make changes.

An arrogant person might say, "I don't need to ask anyone for a kiss or anything else. Everyone wants to be with me."

You could respond nicely by saying, "If everyone wants to be with you, then why are you afraid to ask before doing something with the person? If they want you, they will say 'Yes.' Are you afraid they are going to say 'No'? Are you afraid someone might actually not want to be with you? If you really believe what you are telling me—that everyone wants you—you'll ask next time."

Challenge yourself to help people see the faults in their thought processes. Do not be a bystander to unhealthy behaviors. Make a difference!

Technology

Technology can have a huge influence on relationships, including the way many people pursue relationships and engage in sexual intimacy. Each day, more technological avenues are being paved for helping people meet and form connections virtually (emotional and sexual). At no cost, you can now communicate daily with partners hundreds or thousands of miles away.

Some relationships start in the virtual world and then move to the physical world of being in-person. Some relationships start in-person and then move to the virtual world. Often, relationships incorporate both the virtual world and the in-person physical world. (You text your partner during the day about the two of you getting together later that night).

The new "normal" of relationships is that there is no "normal" relationship. Each relationship is unique, whether the relationship exists online, through texting, through communicating via an app, using the latest technology, or thriving without any integration of technology.

People in virtual relationships feel all the same emotions as people in physical, in-person relationships. Partners feel attraction, love, hurt, and disappointment. Whether you are dating 100 percent virtually or you are using technology to enhance your in-person relationship, you and your partner deserve to be treated with every element of respect and dignity we've already discussed in this book.

With the integration of technology come new ways for predators to target others. Sadly, often these predators disguise themselves as caring, loving partners. Here are two common examples:

From Personal Sharing to Pornography

When partners are communicating virtually, often they still want to "see" each other. After establishing a comfort level, one person may start to request that the partner send a sexually explicit picture and/ or video. If the person does not want to send the picture, sadly, some partners will use guilt, coercion, and pressure to get what they want. (Example: "If you won't send me a picture, I'm going to tell everyone you had sex with me.")

This person pressuring the partner is being predatory and is not acting like a caring, respectful partner. This person is trying to get a partner to take sexual actions the partner does not want to take and that are against the partner's will.

Just as you are never obligated to have sex with a partner, you also never owe your partner any intimate photographs you do not want to share. If a minor is portrayed in the images and/ or video, sending the sexually explicit material is the distribution of child pornography—a crime. This can also include minors sending sexually explicit images of other minors. For example, there have been a number of cases in different states where a teen had a photograph that was taken when the couple was in a relationship. Once the two broke up, one of the parties then posted the sexually explicit photographs on the Internet. This is often referred to as revenge porn, and it is both immoral and illegal. In addition, if an adult exposes a minor to porn (example: showing a nude or sexually explicit picture of themselves), many states can prosecute for the crime of exposing a child to pornography as well as other charges such as contributing to the delinquency of a minor.

Possession

A partner may demand that you be available for them at any time— twenty-four hours a day, seven days a week. So you don't miss their texts or video calls, they may ask you to stay at home and not go out. They may also demand that if you do go out, you constantly text them pictures of where you are and whom you are with in order to keep tabs on you. This behavior is controlling and possessive—it can lead to stalking.

No partner has the right to track your every move and/or decision. You are an independent person who deserves to live in freedom.

Deception

Technology makes it easy for people to pretend to be someone they are not. If you are in a 100 percent virtual relationship, a partner may use deception to draw you in closer and to make you feel safer. They may use pictures of other people and tell you the images are of themselves. They may lie about a multitude of aspects of their personal selves to paint a false picture of whom they actually are. This person is being predatory by relying on deception to gain your trust and give you a sense of feeling safe.

You deserve to be with a partner who is honest and authentic.

Theft

If you do take photographs and/or video footage of yourself and someone steals the materials from you, the person stealing is the person who is engaging in the wrongful behavior. You may have heard about a celebrity's phone or computer being hacked into and that action resulting in sexually explicit pictures of the celebrity being distributed. This behavior by the hacker is theft and a complete invasion of privacy.

If someone took pictures outside the house of another person's bathroom as that person undressed, we all know such behavior would be wrong and illegal. Breaking into someone's computer or phone to steal private images and/or video is no different. When you hear about such hacking cases, put the responsibility for the crime on the criminal—not the victim.

Being in a virtual relationship or using technology in a relationship does not change the rules of dating. The same rules that apply to an in-person relationship apply to one that uses technology. You never have to send pictures or video. You do not have to engage in any activities online that make you uncomfortable. You have the right to say, "No" at any point—regardless of whether you've said "Yes" previously and/or engaged in similar behavior in the past. You are allowed to live your life. No partner has the right to tell you what you can and can't do. You never owe your partner any form of sexual pleasure or gratification. In a completely virtual relationship, you have the right to refuse to meet your partner in-person if you do not feel comfortable. You have the right to end the relationship at any point for any reason.

CHAPTER 9: WHAT INFLUENCES YOU?

Remember this:

- Be yourself!
- Stay away from the games people play.
- Understand that a sober you is likely to make the best choices.
- Be aware at parties, concerts, and events.
- Respect your own and the other person's rights at all times, in both the virtual word and the physical in-person world.

Try this:

Write down more ways friends can be bad influences on your dating life. Then decide how you are going to block out those negative influences.

Bonus

 Strictly Students: Get your "Party Pact" at www.canikissyou.com/students.

 Parents' Pointers: For your son or daughter, make sure you use the "Pickup Plan" at www.canikissyou.com/parents.

 Teachers' Tool: Discover the "Heard – Seen – Done" exercise at www.canikissyou.com/educators.

my**NOTES**:

10

Students of Life
School Is In

A re you a student of life? Are you constantly learning from the people around you? Each person's environment can contribute to their views of dating, relationships, and respect for others. When chosen correctly, your words and actions can help build a more positive atmosphere for everyone.

Language

Are you aware of the impact your words have on others? Awareness is more than listening and paying attention to the people around you. Awareness includes listening and paying attention to what you personally say and do. Do you laugh at jokes based on disrespect or filled with a double standard toward men and women (one standard for men, a different one for women)? When hearing such a joke, what do you do? Instead of the joke being sexist, what if the joke were racist in nature? Would you act differently?

> You walk into a room and see a group of people talking to each other. One person, Emerson, is telling everyone a joke.
> You join the group. The joke is racist and in bad taste. Everyone around you is laughing, but you don't want to laugh. Instead, you smile to avoid feeling out of place. Since

everyone is laughing, Emerson continues with the racist jokes. When everyone else laughs, you continue to smile after each joke.

Are you a racist? You didn't speak out. By smiling, you appeared to approve of the jokes. By doing so, you promoted racist thoughts and stereotypes. Are you saying, "It was just a joke"?

Sexual Harassment

Harmful jokes can create an atmosphere of fear and intimidation for people offended by the joke or attacked in the joke. While most people know racist jokes can be damaging and are disrespectful, many people consider sexist jokes to be "okay." A sexist joke is a joke that makes fun of gender and/or sexual orientation. Think of all the "blonde" jokes you have heard in your lifetime. The majority of sexist jokes are based around negative stereotypes about women.

How can blonde jokes or other sexist jokes cause harm?

A blonde goes to school. By the age of fifteen, the blonde has heard scores of "dumb blonde" jokes. Does this repetition affect the blonde? Yes. Would it affect you? Here is a challenge for you:

As you are walking into school, your friend approaches you and says, "What has happened to you? Your looks have gone downhill." What would you think? When you walk by a mirror, would you take a second look at yourself to see whether the person was right? Later that day, another friend says, "What are you eating or doing to yourself? You just don't look the same anymore." After this comment, how long do you stare in the mirror? Now, two friends have made comments to you. Do you start to question your appearance or your value? You only heard two comments, and you were affected to some degree.

Words can be brutal and damaging. Harassment can occur anywhere: in your home, at school, at work, on a team, and many other places. Harassment is making someone feel intimidated, fearful, or uncomfortable due to your words or actions.

How about this?

Write down every possible example you have seen of harassment at school, work, and home. Be sure to include harassing comments to, and from, all genders.

Example No. 1

You were walking down the school hallway when you heard a group say to one student, "You're the one with the big... (fill in the blank)." Can that comment make someone feel uncomfortable?

Example No. 2

At a high school, a group of seniors yell out to a younger student, "When are you going to hit puberty? You look like a sixth grader in the showers." How would the younger student feel?

What does "actions" mean? If you wanted to intimidate someone, you would not need to talk. You could stare the person down. You could stalk a person. You could continually invade a person's personal space. A group of people could constantly block another person from trying to get somewhere.

During a class, Phoenix notices a classmate staring at a specific area of Phoenix's body. In the hallway, Phoenix catches the same person staring at the same place on Phoenix's body. When Phoenix leaves the school late at night, Phoenix sees the person over near Phoenix's car. Does Phoenix have a legitimate reason to fear the other person? The person never verbally said anything, but the person's actions caused Phoenix to be intimidated and uncomfortable.

You are accountable for your words and your actions. When you hear a sexist joke, how can you use that moment as a learning opportunity for the people around you? Combining a compliment with a question is the best way to open another person's mind. For example, as soon as Addison tells the sexist joke, say, "Addison, I need to talk to you for just a second. Can I talk with you away from the group?" You don't want to embarrass Addison. Doing so will only lead Addison to become defensive. Once the two of you are away from the crowd, nicely ask, "You have always been good at making people laugh. I was just wondering why you felt the need to tell a sexist joke. What if the joke was about someone you really cared about?"

Sexual orientation can often be the center of jokes. One person is heard and seen mocking a specific sexual orientation—even mimicking a stereotype of how a person of that sexual orientation may carry themself.

Help the person recognize the impact their sexist jokes or comments have on others. The words and actions we choose help create the environment we live in. Build healthier gender relations for everyone by eliminating harmful language and insinuations from our conversations.

Is speaking out easy? Not always, but making the right choices helps improve relationships among all genders and sexual orientations. Speak out against unhealthy "norms." Knowing that you have helped another person is both satisfying and fulfilling.

Friends Act Like Friends—The Buddy System

A friend is a person who cares about you and looks out for your best interests. A friend does not take advantage of you. Sadly, many sexual assaults are committed by a person the survivor considered to be a friend. Always honor your friend's boundaries and treat your friend with the utmost respect.

If you go to a party, a club, or an event, go with a group of friends. Don't only accompany each other to the location of the party or event. Stay together throughout the event. Create a "buddy system" where each person has at least one friend who promises to help keep an eye out for them. You make a commitment to each other to take any actions necessary to protect each other.

You only leave the party with your buddy. You do not let your buddy leave the party with a different person. This rule is the one policy friends break the most often. Do not break this rule. Do whatever it takes to make your buddy leave with you. Recognize that when friends are drinking or "having fun," they may forget the agreement that was made and you may end up being the "bad guy" at the moment. Think about whether you would let friends get in a car and drive drunk. Because of the potential danger involved, most of us are willing to be considered the "bad guy" by our friend and will take the car keys away from a drunk person to keep them from driving under the influence.

Friends take care of their friends.

One way to help each friend understand the importance of the buddy system is to have a buddy dinner. Invite all of the friends you want involved over for dinner and talk about protecting each other. Let people ask questions and listen to their comments. Explain why the "buddy system" is vitally important. Once everyone agrees, have everyone commit to the buddy system.

Discuss the dangers of strangers at a party. If a person at a party wants to be with you or get to know you, have the person call you the next day. Let the person ask you out for a date!

Discuss the importance of not letting an intoxicated person go home with anyone other than the people they arrived with. Likewise, do not let the intoxicated person bring a date home. Help your friends stay away from doing harm to another person. If a friend wants to go out with a certain person at a party, have your friend get the person's phone number. By doing so, your friend can call the person the next day when both people are sober and of sound mind.

The Double Standard

Why do many people "look down" on women who are sexually active but not men? The double standard. Our society has a different set of rules based on one's gender. We praise men for the same acts we ridicule and disrespect women and other genders for. Men are applauded for having lots of sexual partners, whereas women are called "sluts."

Listen for people expressing the double standard. If you hear a comment like, "The little slut slept with . . . ," ask the person, "What makes her a slut?" The person will probably tell you, "She sleeps around with so many guys." Point out the double standard by saying, "If the guy wanted to sleep with her, doesn't that make him a slut?"

The double standard has become ingrained in our society. You can hear someone talk about a woman by saying, "The little slut got an 'A' on her test." You are not likely to hear someone talk about a man by saying, "Did you hear he got an 'A'? What a little 'ho' he is." Neither the comments about the woman or the man make sense, yet our society accepts the comment that sexually degrades the woman. In your everyday conversations, listen for the double standard. Hold all genders to an equal standard of treating one another with value and not judgment.

 How about this?

Write down every social norm you can think of for women. Then, try to find the opposite standard for men. Switch the "stereotypical" roles. Is there a double standard for genders other than men and women? Do we treat trans individuals differently?

Example

Write all the negative names for women who are sexually assertive. Then, write all the negative names for men who are sexually assertive. "Slut," "ho," and "tramp," are just a few of the words people use about women who are sexually active. For men, what will you come up with? The words must be completely negative (just like the words for the women were).

Privacy

Respect other people's privacy and sexuality. Do not spread rumors about another person's sexuality or sexual behavior. Do not brag about your own sexual relationships. Bragging is a sign of arrogance and shows no respect for your partner. Talking about other people only leads to their reputations and images being damaged. Have respect for yourself and your partner.

Use Logic

When you hear people discussing sexual issues or stereotypes, apply logic to the conversation. Frequently, our society belittles individuals who choose to abstain from sexual activity. If you examine the logic of a person who chooses to abstain, you often see a person who has set and stood by a value. Logic would tell us to respect this person for making a strong choice. Use logic.

You can make a difference in changing our society's view of sexual assault, survivors, dating, communication, and respect by getting involved in your community. Join your state's coalition against sexual assault. Start an organization in a local school or on a college campus.

Get Involved

Start your own local movement. Share The Date Safe Project motto of **"Ask First. Respect the Answer."** Inspire all genders to work together to educate others. Ask professionals to present workshops. Produce a weekly or monthly YouTube show on important issues concerning your organization's efforts to make a difference.

Here is a good start-up list of people to invite:

- A representative from your local rape crisis center.
- Health teachers and counselors.
- Student peer educators from schools and colleges.
- Local authorities.
- Friends and peers.
- General public—Send press releases to local newspapers and provide public announcements for schools.

To learn more about starting a local movement, visit www.DateSafeProject.org and go into the "Students Only" section of the website to find out more about getting involved.

On the site, you will also find posters, educational tools, articles, videos, eye-catching shirts and shorts, and many more ideas to help you make a positive influence in your local community.

Pledge for Action

What about making a difference throughout the world? How often do you receive junk email (spam) trying to get you to click on a useless or even harmful link. What if you could send an email that actually helped changed lives? The Pledge for Action encourages people to make a caring commitment to their friends, family, and peers.

How do you put the Pledge for Action into an email and get people to sign it? Go to www.DateSafeProject.org and click on "Live the Movement." Choose to "Take the Pledge" and then share the pledge with everyone you know.. Start creating change today.

Talking with Your Elders

"Times were different back in my day. Men always showed respect toward women."

Have you ever heard an elder make the above type of comment? Men respected women? Women couldn't vote for hundreds of years. On a date, men would choose and order their date's meal for the evening. He would decide what she was going to eat. These "old" ideas of respect were misguided. Plus, the entire discussion is heteronormative (assumes everyone is heterosexual). In reality, sexual disrespect has been ingrained in our society for centuries. Today, you have the opportunity to help improve respect for all genders. Accept this task with vigor and pride.

PLEDGE FOR ACTION

I, _____, pledge to do my best to help my family, friends, and peers in potentially dangerous situations in which drugs, alcohol, a violent person, or other threats to their safety and well-being are present. I will do this by having the focus and self-control necessary to remain aware of my surroundings, the wisdom to identify dangerous situations, and the courage to take action in confronting my friends when their judgment is impaired.

I recognize that these dangerous situations may arise at times when people feel safe and comfortable, such as at bars, parties (especially when alcohol is influencing the situation and a person is trying to "hook up" with another individual), or in the context of a romantic relationship. I realize that it may not always be easy to help people from being harmed in these situations, but by remaining watchful and showing care and concern, I may help to prevent a sexual assault from occurring.

I understand that the only person responsible for a sexual assault is the person who engages in sexual contact without the consent of the other person. Through my own positive words, actions, and beliefs, I am taking the responsibility of helping to end sexual assault. I will share with people the importance of consent and the need to obtain consent from your partner by asking first. I will treat all survivors of sexual assault with respect and admiration. I will inform all of my family, friends, and peers that, "If anyone ever has or ever does sexually touch you without your consent, I will fully support you. I will always be here for you. Always (from simply listening to helping you seek the proper support from professionals)!" During the next twenty-four hours, I will start putting this pledge into action by saying these words to at least three people.

Sexual assault is a horrific and traumatic crime. My active commitment to this project will help reduce the violence in my community and create a safer atmosphere for everyone.

Signature _____ Date_____

Think about what you do have in common with the older generation. Did they get nervous before a date? Were they worried about what their date was going to think about them? Did they wonder how the date was going to end? Everyone has experienced these feelings of dating anxiety.

Ask questions in a respectful manner. Talk without being overly blunt. Do not outwardly ask about very private and intimate moments. While you may be trying to learn from the older person's experiences, it will appear you are just trying to pry into their personal life to embarrass them.

Start by asking your elders simple questions like the following:

- **"How did you approach a date?"**
- **"What do you think is the most important lesson to remember when dating?"**
- **"If you could do it all over again, what would you change about the way you dated?"**

Elders can provide you with fantastic life lessons to use in your dating life.

Dating and relationships are two of the few experiences in life where you can experience the wide range of emotion, from fear to pure joy and happiness. Violence, disrespect, and pain do not belong on any date or in any relationship.

Each person can help change the atmosphere toward sexual assault in our culture. With the knowledge and understanding you have, you can challenge the harmful thoughts of others. You can engage individuals in conversations. You can bring the word "respect" to the forefront of relationships. You can inspire admiration and compassion for survivors. You can make dating healthier and more fun. You can help reduce the occurrence of sexual assault. By doing so, you can change the lives of many.

Be responsible. Make a difference!

CHAPTER 10: STUDENTS OF LIFE

Remember this:

- Stop sexism from spreading.
- Listen for and eliminate harassment.
- Speak out to keep schools safe.
- Create a "buddy" system.
- Demolish the double standard.
- Start a local movement.
- Take the Pledge for Action.
- Connect with your elders and learn.
- Get involved.
- Make a difference!

Try this:

Write down exactly what you are going to do to make a difference. There is only one rule. Start taking the action today.

Post #CanIKissYou to Facebook, Instagram or Twitter and Get a Chance to Win DSP Product!

Share pics with the hashtag #CanIKissYou of yourself with the book and/or wearing The Date Safe Project clothing. Doing so will put you in the mix for the potential to win more fun items from The Date Safe Project throughout the year!

Bonus

 Strictly Students: Start making a difference with your friends *today*. Go to: www.canikissyou.com/students. Start a local movement at your school.

 Parents' Pointers: Imagine having every parent teaching the right messages to their children. Your job would be *much* easier. Give all your child's friends the chance to learn the messages in this book by bringing a sensational program to your school and community. Find out more at www.canikissyou.com/parents.

 Teachers' Tool: Keep the message going all year. Hear exactly what to say to your students when real cases break in the media, especially with all the celebrity news nowadays. Go to www.canikissyou.com/educators.

my**NOTES**:

Suggested Reading

To see a complete list of resources, visit www.DateSafeProject.org.

Berkowitz, Alan. *Men and Rape: Theory, Research, and Prevention Programs in Higher Education.* Hoboken, NJ: Jossey-Bass, 1994.

Boumil, Marcia Mobilia and Joel Friedman. *Date Rape: The Secret Epidemic.* Deerfield Beach, FL: Health Communications, 1996.

Buchwald, Emilie. *Transforming a Rape Culture.* Minneapolis, MN: Milkweed Editions, 1995.

Byers, E. Sandra and Lucia F. O'Sullivan. *Sexual Coercion in Dating Relationships.* New York, NY: The Haworth Press, 1996.

Carter, Christine, ed. *The Other Side of Silence: Women Tell About Their Experiences with Date Rape.* Gilsum, NH: Avocus, 1995.

Domitrz, Mike. *Voices of Courage: Inspiration from Survivors of Sexual Assault.* Greenfield, WI: Awareness Publications, 2005.

Funk, Rus Ervin. *Stopping Rape: A Challenge for Men.* Gabriola Island, Brit. Col., Canada: New Society Publications, 1993.

Johnson, Scott A. *Man to Man: When Your Partner Says No—Pressured Sex & Date Rape.* Brandon, VT: Safer Society Press, 1992.

Johnson, Scott A. *When "I Love You" Turns Violent: Emotional and Physical Abuse in Dating Relationships.* Far Hills, NJ: New Horizon Press, 1993.

Katz, Jackson. *The Macho Paradox: Why Some Men Hurt Women and How All Men Can Help.* Naperville, IL: Sourcebooks, 2006.

Kilmartin, Chris and Alan Berkowitz. *Sexual Assault in Context: Teaching College Men About Gender.* n.p. FL: Learning Publications, 2000.

Kivel, Paul. *Men's Work: How to Stop the Violence That Tears Our Lives Apart.* Center City, MN: Hazelden, 1999.

Lefkowitz, Bernard. *Our Guys: The Glen Ridge Rape and the Secret Life of the Perfect Suburb.* Berkeley, CA: U of California P, 1997.

Levine, Robert Barry. *When You Are the Partner of a Rape or Incest Survivor: A Workbook for You.* Searcy, AR: Resource Publications, 1996.

Levy, Barrie. *Dating Violence: Young Women in Danger.* Seattle, WA: Seal Press, 1991.

Lindquist, Scott. *The Date Rape Prevention Book: The Essential Guide for Girls and Women.* Naperville, IL: Sourcebooks, 2000.

Raine, Nancy Venable. *After Silence: Rape and My Journey Back.* New York, NY: Three Rivers Press, 1999.

Sanday, Peggy Reeves. *A Woman Scorned: Acquaintance Rape and Trial.* New York, NY: Doubleday, 1996.

Sebold, Alice. *Lucky: A Memoir.* New York, NY: Back Bay Books, 2002.

Warshaw, Robin. *I Never Called It Rape.* New York, NY: Harper & Row Publishers, 1988.

Winkler, Kathleen. *Date Rape: A Hot Issue.* New York, NY: Enslow Publishers, 1999.

About the Author

Mike Domitrz is an internationally renowned speaker, subject matter expert, trainer, and a critically acclaimed author who has devoted his life to reducing sexual assault by helping society transform our culture to one built on respect and consent.

After the devastation of his sister being sexually assaulted in 1989, Mike was determined to make a difference. While still in college, he created and designed his own interactive presentation, "Can I Kiss You? Dating, Communication, Respect & Sexual Assault Awareness." His goal was to open the eyes of people toward this important societal issue.

Today, Mike speaks to tens of thousands each year. His impact on audiences has made him one of the most sought-after subject matter experts and presenters in schools, on college campuses, at educational conferences, and on military installations around the world.

He created "The Date Safe Project" to launch national initiatives and produce educational products to assist students, parents, educators, military leaders, and survivors across the globe (www.DateSafeProject.org).

Media and news outlets appreciate Mike's unique and helpful insights, including Dateline NBC's "My Kid Would Never Do That" special series that featured Mike as an expert on its episode addressing sexual assault, consent, and bystander intervention.

To learn more about Mike, visit: www.DateSafeProject.org

Bring Mike to Speak

To schedule Mike for a keynote speech, assembly, convocation, seminar, workshop, convention, or training session, contact:

The Date Safe Project
Toll-Free: (800) 329-9390
www.DateSafeProject.org

When students, educators, administrators, counselors, parents, military leaders, and organizations hear Mike speak, they stand together in praise of his message and his approach. He exposes the problem and then inspires people with simple solutions!

In each program, Mike shares specific skill sets every person can implement immediately in their lives and can share with those around them.

Plus, Mike will customize the entire program to fit the needs of your audience and your organization.

On-Demand Video
Can't make it to a live event with Mike Domitrz? Then join him online by watching one of his On-Demand video series.

Visit Mike on the Internet at: www.DateSafeProject.org
Email: mike.d@datesafeproject.org

Attend a Live Conference

After seeing Mike speak, audience members will often ask, "How do I learn to engage those I lead with the passion and direction Mike did today? How can I help people make positive behavioral changes in just one hour?"

A great choice is to attend a live training conference hosted and facilitated by Mike Domitrz.

Each year, The Date Safe Project hosts live conferences and trainings designed to help individuals further grow in their personal and professional lives.

Mike uncovers the techniques and strategies that have helped him become so successful at reaching difficult audiences. Then, he reveals how you can use these same methods to help others.

For more information on attending a conference or in-person training with Mike Domitrz, go to:

www.DateSafeProject.org/conference

More from Mike Domitrz

HELP! My Teen is Dating.
Real Solutions to Tough Conversations
By Mike Domitrz

The ultimate DVD for parents! Discover the proper way to prepare your children for the dangers of dating and the "hook-up" fad in today's sexual culture. In this two-hour interactive DVD (also available via On-Demand Video), you will learn the keys to engaging your child in powerful and fun conversations on dating, intimacy, and sexual choices. **Available at: www.HelpMyTeenIsDating.com**

Voices of Courage: Inspiration from Survivors of Sexual Assault
Edited by Mike Domitrz

From tragedy to triumph, inspiring lessons unfold in this one-of-a-kind book by twelve survivors of sexual assault. This eye-opening journal of personal growth and recovery is available in paperback, eBook, and audio book (listen to the actual twelve survivors). The eBook and audio book can be downloaded for **FREE at: www.VoicesOfCourage.com**

Get Social & Join the Conversation:

- ▶ youtube.com/DateSafeProject
- f facebook.com/DateSafe
- 🐦 @DateSafeProject

Visit Us Online at
www.DateSafeProject.com!

Spread the important and powerful message of "Asking First," intervening, and supporting survivors through educational materials produced by The Date Safe Project. DSP also offers a thriving content hub on topics relevant to you updated daily, including an "Ask Mike" platform where you can get your questions answered directly by Mike Domitrz via a video answer!" From T-shirts to wristbands, from temporary tattoos to posters, and from in-person training events to online learning courses, find the perfect resources to share these messages with family, friends, and your entire community. Visit: www. DateSafeProject.org

Can I Kiss You?

Temporary Tattoo

Post #CanIKissYou to Facebook, Instagram or Twitter and Get a Chance to Win DSP Product!

Share pics with the hashtag #CanIKissYou of yourself with the book and/or wearing The Date Safe Project clothing. Doing so will put you in the mix for the potential to win more fun items from The Date Safe Project throughout the year!

The Date Safe Project
P.O. Box 20906
Greenfield, WI 53228
www.DateSafeProject.org
Info@datesafeproject.org
800-329-9390: toll-free
920-326-3687: local